HEADSTONE'S FOLLY

A JOHN HEADSTON MYSTERY

OTHER MYSTERIES BY ROBERT J. RANDISI

Hitman with a Soul Trilogy
Upon My Soul
Souls of the Dead
Envy the Dead

The Johnny Headston Series
The Headstone Detective Agency
Headstone's Folly
Blood on a Headstone (*)

The Miles Jacoby Series
Eye in the Ring
The Steinway Collection
Full Contact
Separate Cases
Hard Look
Stand Up

The Nick Delvecchio Series
No Exit from Brooklyn
The Dead of Brooklyn
The End of Brooklyn

The Gil & Claire Hunt Series
Murder is the Deal of the Day
The Masks of Auntie Laveau
Same Time, Same Murder

The Joe Keough Series
Alone with the Dead
In the Shadow of the Arch
Blood on the Arch
East of the Arch
Arch Angels
Back to the Arch

The Dennis McQueen Series
The Turner Journals
Cold-Blooded

The Rat Pack Series
Everybody Kills Somebody Sometime
Luck be a Lady, Don't Die
Hey You, with the Gun in Your Hand
You're Nobody til Somebody Kills You
I'm a Fool to Kill You
Fly Me to the Morgue
It was a Very Bad Year
You Make Me Feel So Dead
The Way You Die Tonight
I Only Have Lies for You
That Old Dead Magic

The Auggie Velez/Nashville Series
The Honky Tonk Big Hoss Boogie
The Last Sweet Song of Hammer Dylan

Stand Alone Crime Novels
The Disappearance of Penny
The Ham Reporter
Curtains of Blood
The Offer
The Bottom of Every Bottle
The Picasso Flop

Collections
Delvecchio's Brooklyn
The Guilt Edge

(*) Coming Soon

ROBERT J. RANDISI

HEADSTONE'S FOLLY

A JOHN HEADSTON MYSTERY

DOWN&OUT
BOOKS

Down & Out Books
3959 Van Dyke Road, Suite 265
Lutz, FL 33558
DownAndOutBooks.com

Cover design by Melody Designs

ISBN: 1-64396-148-9
ISBN-13: 978-1-64396-148-4

*For Marthayn, comingling my life with yours was no folly.
It was the smartest thing I've ever done.*

PART ONE

ONE

New York City, 2005

I stopped just inside the door of the Headstone Detective Agency and looked at the line of desks, all occupied. Twelve operatives. The twelfth one was a new man, employed only a week earlier. Now, three years after opening, I had my full complement of investigators.

When I first opened the agency three years earlier it was meant to be called the Headston Agency, named after me, John Headston. But when the business cards were printed saying "Headstone" agency, and there were a thousand of them, I decided to let it stand. I even changed the name on the door, adding the "e" myself, which is why it looked slightly different.

I exchanged greetings with the operatives who weren't on the phone, stopped at my secretary, Marlene's desk.

"Messages," she said, handing me a handful of pink slips. She was blond, with big blue eyes magnified by her thick, horn-rimmed glasses which she was always pushing up her nose with one finger.

"Anything urgent?"

"Urgent? No. Important? Yes. Read 'em."

"Yes, ma'am."

I took the messages into my office, sat behind my desk and started going through them. A couple of clients wanted their

3

written reports before they sent a check. That was what Marlene meant by "important." So I spent the next hour preparing bills. It took that long because I preferred to do billing myself rather than have Marlene do it, but that meant a lot of mistakes on my typewriter.

"You know you should let me do that," Marlene said from the door. "Or, at least, get a new typewriter."

"This one is fine."

"It was fine sixty years ago. What you really need in here is a computer."

She opened her mouth to say something else, but then her attention was attracted elsewhere.

"Yikes," she said.

"What?"

"Looks like some new clients. A man and a woman."

"Find out what they want."

"They look like money, Johnny," she said, "and she's a stunner." She turned to leave, closing my door.

I made eight typos on another bill before Marlene knocked and entered.

"So?"

"Did I say money?" she asked. "This guy's loaded, and has a problem."

"What's the problem?"

"He won't tell me," she said. "Just you. And he's willing to pay you a thousand dollars for your time."

"All right, then," I said. "Bring him in."

"I'll bring them both in," Marlene said, "but you have to remember, this is his wife."

"Okay," I said, "husband-and-wife, got it."

"I know how you are with good looking women, Johnny," Marlene said. "If you want this guy's money, you'll have to be careful with his wife."

"What do you think I'm gonna do?" I asked. "Jump over my desk at her?"

4

"When they come in, you'll understand why I'm worried."

Marlene's concern might have had something to do with the fact that I had hit on her the first week she was on the job. She made it clear she didn't date the boss, and that was that. Hey, I like pretty women. And cute women. And beautiful women.

Marlene opened the door. The client's wife qualified for the last group. In fact, she defined it. "Mr. Headston, this is Mister Vincent Balducci, and his wife. Carla."

I stood up, prepared to greet them both, but I have to admit, Carla Balducci took my breath away. I immediately knew why Marlene was worried, and I tried to compose myself.

"Mr. and Mrs. Balducci," I greeted, shaking the man's hand, "please, have a seat."

"Mr. Headston," the man said. He was tall, gray-haired, in his fifties, wearing a suit that cost more than all the furniture in my office.

Carla Balducci simply nodded at me, so I had no voice at that moment to go with the gorgeous violet eyes and lush lips. She had to be about fifteen years younger than her husband, but it was a very well-cared for forty.

I sat down. Tore my eyes away from the lady and asked, "What can I do for you, sir?"

"I own a company," Balducci said, "and somebody is stealin' from me. I want it stopped. You been recommended to me."

"By who?"

"We have a mutual friend named Sugar Garbanzo."

If I needed any more proof that Balducci was connected, that did it. I grew up with Sugar, and when we got old enough, he went the wrong way and I went the right way. At least, it started out that way. Later, the lines started to blur. That was when I decided to leave the police department and open my own shop. I wasn't prepared to go Serpico on anybody's ass.

"How is Sugar?" I asked. "I haven't seen him in a while."

"He's doin' good," Balducci said. "He's out."

"Good to know."

"I told him what I needed and he said you were just enough cop and just enough crook to get it done—for a price."

"Sugar has a lot of faith in my abilities," I said. "Let's just hope he's right."

"I think he is," Mrs. Balducci said. Her husband gave her a quick look. She shrugged. "I can just tell."

Balducci patted her hand, then squeezed it. I had a feeling it meant a lot more than it seemed to.

"Okay, then," I said, rubbing my hands together, "let's get to it. What kind of business are we talking about, and what's been stolen?"

Balducci spoke for the next fifteen minutes. I listened without interrupting. It was usually the best method for getting all the facts. That and a few follow-up questions.

"You're a lawyer, a founding partner of your firm, and somebody is stealing clients?"

"That's about the size of it."

Which explained why he hadn't gone to the police. What was happening wasn't a crime, it was just business.

"I want you to find out who the thief is."

"And then what?"

"Then tell me," he said. "After that, you're done. You bill me, and I'll pay you five grand above the total."

"Five thousand dollars?"

"Bonus."

I looked at Mrs. Balducci, and she raised one eyebrow. Normally, I hate people who can do that, but on her it looked good.

"Who's my contact at your firm?" I asked. "I mean, for information."

"You come up there and I'll introduce you to my secretary. She's it."

"Okay, I'll have one of my operatives—"

"No," Balducci said, "I want you. That's what the bonus is for. I want the main man."

"Well," I said, "all right. I'll come by later today."

"That's good," he said. "I was hoping you'd get started quickly."

They both stood. I tried not to stare at her in front of her husband. He extended his hand and I shook it.

"I'll see you later," he said.

"Mrs. Balducci," I said, looking at his wife. "Nice to meet you."

"It's Carla," she said, putting her hand out, "please."

"Carla."

Balducci took her arm, holding it a little too tight, and led her away. I watched them go out the door, then looked at Marlene, who had her head cocked my way.

"What?"

"I know you," she said. "That woman is trouble, and you can't resist trouble."

"I don't know what you're talking about."

TWO

Three months later...

Trying to find a thief in a law firm is like trying to find a needle in a haystack. And if anybody understands billable hours, it's a lawyer.

"Vincent's been wondering what's taking so long," the woman in my bed said.

I was lying on my back, enjoying the afterglow. We'd been doing this for two of the three months since we met. She was sure Vincent didn't know about us.

"These things take time."

"That's what I've been telling him."

She reached over and started trying to massage new life into my flaccid penis. I'd told her that a man in his mid-thirties needs some time to recover, but she reminded me that she was a woman in her early forties, which meant she was at her sexual peak. I knew that was true because it had been in both *Playboy* and *Cosmo*, but it still didn't seem fair.

"If he ever finds out you're dragging this on so you can keep billing him..."

"...and sleep with his wife," I reminded her.

"...he'll kill you," Carla said.

"I know," I said, "you've told me that before."

"You could've slept with his young secretary, you know,"

8

she said. "Margo sleeps with anyone."

"Twenty-two-year-olds are so boring," I said.

She leaned over and kissed my shoulder. Her paid for, high breasts didn't sag. I didn't mind fake boobs. Not when they were tasteful like hers, rather than huge Anna Nicole Smith specials. The rest of her body was attributed to Pilates and tennis, but the boobs were a gift from her husband.

"She's my official contact," I reminded her, sliding my hand down one of her smooth thighs. "I'm more partial to my unofficial contact."

She pressed her mouth to my ear. "The one who can get you killed?"

"Exactly."

I turned my head to capture her hot mouth with mine. Suddenly, things in her hand were looking more promising.

When I got back to the office half of my guys were out on cases. The others were at their desks, doing their footwork on the phone.

Marlene gave me her disapproving look as she handed me my pink message slips.

"What?"

"Nothing," she said, but she sniffed after it.

"Look," I said, "I've told you nothing's goin' on."

"I know you have," she said, "and I believe you." Another sniff.

I gave up and went into the office. I really didn't need her approval, just her secretarial skills.

I sat behind my desk, put my messages down, leaned back and thought about Carla Balducci. When I wasn't with her that's what I did, thought about her.

We played games the first month—hot looks and lingering handshakes—but we sealed the deal in a hotel the beginning of the second month. We'd been meeting a few times a week since then. She'd been keeping me up to date on her husband's level of frustration, among other things.

Marlene didn't have to tell me I was wrong. I knew it. But Carla had come after me. I learned my lesson long ago about chasing married women. There are plenty of unmarried ones available. But when a classy, beautiful married woman chases you, what're you supposed to do?

I had stacks of files on my desk that had been provided to me by Margo, Vincent Balducci's private secretary. She was a flirty, pretty twenty-two-year-old who was probably sleeping with her boss. I had worked my way through the files, and managed to whittle my suspect list down to three.

I wasn't actually dragging my feet on the case—not really. The three men high on my list just happened to be men that Balducci thought he could trust. He'd want to know for sure which one it was, with no doubt, and as yet I hadn't gotten there. Admittedly, my dalliance with Carla was slowing me down, but that's all it was doing. I'd get there, eventually.

But eventually was coming up fast. Balducci was not going to keep paying me, so I decided that this week I'd have to wrap it up. Also, there was the fact that I wouldn't get the five-grand bonus until the case was over.

It was time to put money before sex.

I looked up and saw Marlene in the doorway.

"What is it?"

"She's on the phone," she said, pulling a face so I'd know who she meant.

"Okay, thanks."

I didn't pick up the extension until she turned and went back to her desk.

"Hello, Carla? What's—"

"I need help, Johnny," she said. "Oh God, I need your help."

"What is it?"

I heard her take a big, shuddering breath, and then she said in a rush, "He's dead!"

THREE

One year later…

It was time, finally, for me to get up on the stand and tell my version. I was allowed to change from my prison orange to a suit—the one I had been wearing when they arrested me.

They walked me into the courtroom and sat me down next to my lawyer, Steve Ryder.

"You sure you wanna do this?" Steve asked.

"I've got to," I said. "They've got to hear my side. You saw her up there with those crocodile tears."

"Not to mention the legs and eyes."

"Come on, Steve," I said. "Not you, too."

"Hey," he said, "I'm not the one who was fucking my client's wife."

"Yeah, yeah…" I said.

"All rise!"

The judge came in and sat while his bailiff reminded us all of his name.

"Mr. Ryder?" Judge Henry Mathis said. "Are you ready with your first witness?"

"Yes, your honor," Steve said, standing. "The defense calls John Headston."

The judge frowned down at something on his desk.

"I thought his name was Headstone."

"No, your honor," Steve said. "that's the name of his agency, the Headstone Detective Agency. His name is Headston."

"Yes, yes, very well," the judge said. "Have him come up."

I went up, put my hand on the Bible and swore to tell the truth. I wasn't sure it was going to be the whole truth, but it would be pretty close.

I sat on the stand and waited.

"Would you please tell the court your name," Steve said.

"John Headston."

"Any middle name?"

"None."

"And you own and operate the Headstone Detective Agency."

"That's right."

"And the lawyer Vincent Balducci was your client...until his murder."

"That's correct."

"A murder you are on trial for."

"Yes."

"All right," Steve said, "suppose we start at the beginning..."

I was on the stand for over an hour, telling the story from the time Balducci and his wife walked into my office, until the time she called me and said she needed me, because her husband was dead. I rushed over there to rescue the damsel in distress, and when I arrived I was arrested for murder...

"So you were not able to tell Mr. Balducci who was stealing his clients before he was killed."

"I was not."

"But you gave the police three names, members of his firm who you suspected."

"Yes."

"And you believe one of those three men killed him."

"Yes."

"And just for the record," Steve finished, "you did not kill him."

"I did not."

Steve turned and looked at the district attorney.

"Your witness."

My lawyer sat, and the DA, George Adamson, stood up, buttoned his jacket, and approached me. He wasn't leaving this thing to any of his ADAs.

"Mr. Headston," he said, "is it true you were sleeping with Carla Balducci?"

"Yes."

"Why should we believe that you did not kill Vincent Balducci?"

"He was going to pay me a five-thousand-dollar bonus, over my fee, when I told him who was stealing his clients. Why would I kill him?"

"You were having an affair with his wife," the DA pointed out, again, looking at the jury to bring that point home. "Why would she say you killed him?"

"One of two reasons," I said. "Either she killed him, or she had a lover who killed him."

"That's right," he said. "You."

"No, not me," I said. "I was the lover who played the sap for her."

"So, let me get this straight," he said. "You're claiming she had two lovers. You and another man, and she and the other man killed her husband and pinned it on you. Is that what you want us to believe?"

"It is."

He folded his arms, looked at the jury, smirked and said, "Prove it."

"From here?" I looked down at the handcuffs I was still wearing.

"Do you expect us to let you go?" he asked.

"I expected the cops to do their job," I said. "They didn't."

"You were a police officer once, were you not?"

"I was."

"Where?"

"In New York."

"How long?"

"Eight years."

"And then you quit?"

"That's right."

"At what rank?"

"Detective Third Grade."

"After eight years you were a detective?" he said. "You advanced fairly quickly. Why did you quit?"

I hesitated.

"Mr. Headston? Why did you quit? Or were you fired?"

"I quit."

"Then for the third time...why?"

"Corruption."

"You were corrupt?"

"No," I said, "but it was going on around me. I didn't want to have anything to do with it, so I quit and opened my own shop."

"Ah, so you were an honest cop."

"Yes."

"In a department of corrupt ones."

"There were...bad apples."

"Why not work to weed them out, then?"

"That didn't work so good for Frank Serpico," I said. "I decided to just leave."

"So you're an honest man."

"Yes."

"Then why sleep with a client's wife?"

"That was morally wrong," I said, "not dishonest."

"Isn't your license under review for sleeping with a client's wife?" he asked. "And for possibly killing a client?"

"It is."

"So you still say you're honest?"

"Yes."

He looked at the jury again.

"An honest man who is in danger of losing his license and going to prison."

"Objection!" Steve said, and I was wondering what had taken him so long. "That's not a question. The DA is badgering the witness."

"I don't think he is," the judge said. "Your objection is over-ruled, but Mr. Ryder is correct about one thing, Mr. Adamson. That was not a question."

"I apologize, your honor," Adamson said. "I'll withdraw it."

"The jury will disregard the district attorney's last remark," the judge said. He looked at Adamson. "Continue. And try to stay on track."

"Yes, your honor."

He turned to face me again.

FOUR

"Mrs. Balducci testified you asked her to leave her husband, and when she refused, you came to their home and shot him."

"That's what she said."

"And what do you say?"

"I gave the police my statement."

He looked at the jury and said, "Indulge us."

"Carla called me, said she needed me right away. She said 'he's dead.'"

"Did she say who 'he' was?"

"No," I said, "but I assumed she was talking about her husband."

"Continue, please."

"I hurried to the house, and when I got there Vincent Balducci was lying on the floor, dead. He'd been shot several times."

"And where was Carla?"

"Nowhere."

"How did you get into the house? A lover's key?"

"The front door was open."

"You didn't find that suspicious?" he asked. "An experienced fella like you?"

"I did, but I was worried about Carla."

"Who wasn't there."

"Right."

"But the police were?"

"Right again. Before I could leave they came in and arrested me."

"That's right," Adamson said, "because she called nine-one-one and told them a man named Headston had just killed her husband."

"She lied."

"Oh right, she had one lover kill her husband and frame the other lover."

"Yes."

"How did you end up with the short end of that stick, Mr. Headston?" he asked. "Why weren't you the other lover? Had she ever asked you to kill her husband?"

"No."

"So then you were the sap from the beginning?"

"Looks like it."

"So, rather than arrest you and put you in prison," Adamson said, "we should feel sorry for you. Is that what you want?"

"Between those two things," I answered, "that would be my preference, yes."

"I think that's enough for today," the judge said. "Mr. Adamson, do you have more questions for this witness?"

"Oh, yes, sir, I do."

"Then we'll pick this up at nine tomorrow morning," the judge said. "Court's adjourned."

Before they took me back to a cell for the night they put me in a room with my lawyer.

"Sit, Johnny," Steve said.

There was a long, gleaming wooden table in the center of the room, matching chairs, and books all around us—legal journals.

I sat. Steve sat across from me, opened his briefcase.

"They're offering a deal," he said. "Second degree—"

"No deal," I said.

"You haven't heard—"

"I didn't kill him, Steve, remember?" I said. "So I'm not pleading."

"So we keep going?"

"We keep going," I said.

"Okay." He closed his briefcase and stood up. "I'll see you in the morning, Johnny."

FIVE

Three years later...

I unlocked my office door and, before stepping inside, stared lovingly at that crooked "e" on the end. All twelve desks were empty, except for a layer of dust. Likewise Marlene's desk. I had heard from her while in prison, telling me she couldn't wait any longer and had gotten another job. I gave her my blessing.

My once thriving business was now a huge, empty room with bare desks. The Headstone Agency was pretty much just a headstone.

I went into my office, which smelled musty. I opened a couple of file cabinets, found them mostly empty, except for some old paper clips, an empty bourbon bottle—I know, a PI cliché—and the last page of a few files, with only a line or two on them. Marlene had written me in prison that she had farmed my cases out to other agencies. I told her it was okay—which it was—and that I'd see her soon—but I didn't. It was thirty-eight months before I got out of Sing Sing.

It took that long for the cops to find out who realty killed Vincent Balducci. It was Carla's other lover. Actually, they didn't find him, he finally gave in to three years of guilt and confessed. He said Carla had put him up to it, but by that time Carla was gone and the cops couldn't find her, so they settled for the lover.

They let me out, expunged my record. I was no longer a convicted felon. But I was also no longer a private eye. While in prison my license had been revoked by New York State. Now that I was free, I was going to have to apply to be reinstated. Even though I hadn't committed murder, I had still done a few things that were considered dodgy. They weren't about to just let me back in...

I stared at the three people seated at the table in front of me, two men, one woman, all middle-aged.

"I don't understand," I said to them. "I've been cleared of all charges."

"Of murder, yes," the woman said. She was seated between the two men, and seemed to be in charge. "But there are other... matters."

"Such as?"

"Well, primarily," she said, "the fact that you had an affair with a client's wife."

The two men stared at me and shook their heads. I hadn't been inside long enough to face a parole board, but imagined it would've felt just like this.

"Not very professional behavior, Mr. Headstone," she said.

"It's Headston."

"Really?" She frowned, read her file. "It says 'Headstone Detective Agency.'" She stared at him. "Are you using an assumed name for your business? Because if you are, that would be a problem, as well."

"No, no," I said, "a lot of people make that mistake, and I thought it was a good business name."

"Hmm." She frowned again. "Well, there's still the matter of the illicit affair."

"Illicit?" I said.

"What would you call it?" she asked.

I decided to play up to her.

"Well, I'd call it a mistake," I said, "definitely a mistake."

"Indeed." She closed my folder and looked at me. "I'm afraid we're going to have to keep your license from you a little longer, Mr. Headston."

"How much longer?"

She folded her hands and set them down firmly on my file.

"We'll let you know, Mr. Headston."

Despite the fact that it was going to take time to get my license back, I decided to keep the office. Luckily, it was rent controlled. I was determined that, one day, I'd get my license back, get my business back up and running with butts back in all twelve chairs.

But that was going to take a while. The New York State Division of Licensing Services didn't just hand those things out, willy-nilly. They were pretty much going to make me beg...for a very long time.

I had managed to get the phone service turned back on, so I dialed a number I knew by heart.

"John Headston for Steve Ryder," I said to the secretary who answered.

"Please hold."

After a minute Steve came on.

"Johnny, where are you?"

"My office."

"Your office," he said. "Man, you know you can't be back at work—"

"Relax, relax," I said. "I'm just keepin' the place for when I get my license back."

"Johnny, come on, man, you know that could take a while," Steve warned.

"I'm well aware, Steve," I said. "That's why I thought maybe you could use some help."

"Me? What kind of help?"

"You know," I said, "with the investigations on some of your cases."

"Johnny, I have my guys—hey, I tried to hire you once but you took the high road on me. My cases weren't big enough for you. You remember that?"

"I do remember," I said, "but who did I call when I needed my life saved?"

"Okay, look," Steve said, after a moment, "maybe I can use you, but you're not licensed. I'll have to put you on staff as a...researcher, legal assistant, or something. We'll have to figure it out."

"I appreciate it, Steve," I said. "Now that I'm out I'll buy you a steak at Peter Luger's."

"That's a deal."

"But maybe..."

"What?"

"...you could give me a little advance?"

PART TWO

SIX

The present...

There was a girl on *Saturday Night Live* who used to say, "I'm fifty and I can kick."

Well, I was fifty, and I was getting kicked.

The man I was serving the papers on had taken umbrage and, along with his two friends, had decided to kick the shit out of me. A crowd of people gathered in front of the Tenth Avenue bar to watch, and before long they started to cheer...

I woke up in an alley, sore as hell but apparently still in one piece. Luckily, it didn't seem as if any of the three half-drunk dudes had kicked me in the head. Getting to my feet I felt the most pain in my ribs. Both my trousers and my jacket had been torn.

I needed a drink, but I couldn't go into the same bar where three patrons had just kicked my ass, so I walked a couple of blocks before stopping in another Tenth Avenue gin mill.

I had a shot of whiskey and a beer, otherwise known as a boilermaker. It was a drink that was pretty much a staple in these West side bars. But certainly not trendy, in the high-toned bars frequented by millennials, these days.

"Rough day?" the bartender asked.

"You don't know the half of it."

That was it, he was done consoling me and moved on to the next customer.

I decided against a second and left, went back to my Fifth Avenue office. There was aspirin in my top desk drawer, and I needed it badly.

As I entered I tried not to think about the twelve empty desks and instead looked at the one occupied one.

"Jesus," Ally said, jumping up from her chair, "what happened to you?"

"I'm all right," I said, as she came alongside me. "I just need some aspirin."

"I'll get you water."

She rushed to the small refrigerator she had contributed to the office furniture and brought a bottle of cold water to my desk as I dropped into my chair.

"Thanks." I accepted it, gratefully, washed down a handful of aspirin.

"You're only supposed to take a couple of those," she warned.

It was fall, so she was wearing long sleeves, covering her collection of tattoos.

"You're gonna need a new jacket," she said.

I looked down at the dirty, torn sports jacket I was wearing.

"Can't this be cleaned and mended?"

"Mended?" she asked. "Is that even a word anybody uses, anymore? No, this jacket is for the trash. Goodwill wouldn't even take it." She peered under my desk. "Looks like the pants match. You better change before your meeting."

"What meeting?"

She handed me a message slip.

"That one."

The slip said I was meeting someone named Mrs. Pennyworth at five p.m. for dinner at Keens Steakhouse, on West Thirty-Sixth Street.

"She's gonna get a table at Keens?" I asked.

"Apparently."

Before famed food writer and chef Anthony Bourdain died he once said that you could probably go to Keens in fifty years and it would still look the same. I wouldn't know, because I'd never been able to get a table there.

"You're gonna have to go home and change," Ally said.

"I have a change of clothes here," I said. "I'll just wash up first." I put the message slip down. "When did she call?"

"Right after you left to go and serve your papers," she said. "Who beat your ass?"

"The last one I went to, Raymond Dexter," I said, standing and removing my jacket. She took it from me so I wouldn't hang it up in my closet. "I didn't find him home, but a neighbor told me where he hung out."

"A bar?" she asked. "You went to the guy's bar? Didn't you think he'd be half in the bag by the time you got to him? Telling a drunk 'you've been served' is a sure way to get your ass kicked."

"Thanks for the warning."

As I headed for the bathroom she yelled, "Change your shirt, too!"

Keens was a hot spot before Bourdain pushed it on TV, so now it was almost impossible to get a table. This lady must have some serious gelt.

"Sir?" the maître d' asked, as I entered. "Do you have a reservation?" He looked me up and down, frowned at my back-up jacket.

"I'm meeting Mrs. Pennyworth," I said. "I'm sure she has a reservation."

"The Pennyworths have a regular table," the stocky man said, as if that was something I should've known. "Are you Mr....Headstone?"

"Headston," I said. "John Headston."

He looked down at his book.

"Yes, well...this way."

He led me through the restaurant filled with diners to a back table where a woman was seated with her back to me.

"Mrs. Pennyworth," he said, "your guest is here."

"Thank you, Charles," she said.

I went on the other side of the table to sit across from her, with my back to the wall, when I saw her face.

"Oh, I'm gonna need a drink," I said.

Mrs. Pennyworth, who I knew as Carla Balducci, said, "Hello, Johnny."

SEVEN

I sat down across from her. She looked good, even though I knew she had to be in her mid-fifties by now.

"You look good, John," she said.

"Bullshit," I said. "My hair's receding and my belly isn't. On the other hand, you look fabulous." She was wearing expensive sunglasses, but what I could see of her face was smooth and beautiful.

"Thank you," she said. "I try."

A small, older waiter came over, wearing a white shirt and black vest.

"Winston, we'll each have a vodka martini with two olives."

"Yes, madam."

It was what we used to drink when we'd meet in a bar or restaurant, back when we were sleeping together.

"So who's this Pennyworth guy, Carla?" I asked. "Another sap?"

"Please," she said. "I go by Constance, now, Constance Pennyworth."

"So you married this one?" I asked. "And now you want to kill him?"

"Oh my God, Johnny, what an imagination you have."

"Imagination?" I asked. "You killed your last husband, or don't you remember that I went to prison for it?"

29

"I didn't kill Vincent, Johnny," she said, "and I know you didn't, either. That was Philip."

Philip was Philip Ivy, the lover—sap—who had finally confessed.

"That didn't stop you from letting me take the fall for it," I reminded her.

"I was afraid Philip was going to kill me, too," she said. "I ran. I'm sorry." She reached out for my hand, which I withdrew. "Come on, Johnny. Don't be like that. We were in love, once."

"You never loved me, Carla," I said. "You were just using me."

She looked around and said, "Constance, please."

"Okay, Constance," I said. "How long have you had Pennyworth on the hook?"

"When I ran from here I went to Aruba," she said. "We met there, fell in love, and got married."

"In what? Three months?"

"Two."

"A whirlwind romance."

Winston brought the drinks and Carla/Constance told him we'd order soon.

"How old is he?" I asked.

"Alan is a little older than me," she said. "He's seventy-five." More like twenty years older than she was.

I sipped my drink.

"Want to tell me why I'm here?"

"Well, for one thing," she said, removing her glasses, "when's the last time you had a good steak?"

Constance had the New York strip and I decided to go for the prime rib.

"I need your help, Johnny."

"So you think I shouldn't just turn you over to the police?" I asked.

"The police don't want Constance Pennyworth for anything," she said. "And, as a matter of fact, they don't want Carla Balducci, either."

She was right. The cops were happy to put me away, and then when Philip Ivy confessed they were satisfied with that. They were never looking for Carla.

"Okay," I said, against my better judgment. Besides, I wanted to finish my prime rib. "What's on your mind?"

"Somebody's trying to kill my husband."

"No kidding," I said. "And if he gets killed, you inherit everything, right?"

"Wrong," she said. "He's got two daughters, and he's leaving the bulk of his estate to them when he dies."

"So somebody's trying to kill 'im, and you don't want him dead until you can convince him to change his will."

She smiled. "Right."

"How long have you been married, now?"

"Twelve years."

"And he hasn't changed it, yet?"

"He has," she said. "Twice. And his daughters hate me for it. They don't want him to change it a third time."

"So you think it's one of his daughters who's tryin' to kill him before he can do that?"

"Them or one of their husbands."

Winston came over and looked at my empty plate.

"Dessert, sir?"

"Yes, I'll have Keens' famous coffee cantata." It was the most expensive dessert on their menu.

"Madam?"

"The crème brûlée, Winston."

"Yes, madam. Coffee?"

"Yes, please," she said, "for both of us."

He bowed and backed away, taking our empties with him.

"Johnny," she said, "I need you to find out who it is and stop them."

31

"Have you called the police?"

She squirmed.

"I don't want to do that, for obvious reasons."

"So you're not sure they've stopped looking for Carla Balducci."

She shrugged.

"Even after all these years, I don't want to take any chances," she explained.

"Then why come to New York?"

"My husband comes on business," she said. "I decided to come with him this time, to talk to you."

"Why not hire another agency?" I asked. "My operation is a little shoestring these days."

"I know," she said. "I did my research. You've been struggling since you got your license back. That's why I thought you'd be able to use twenty thousand dollars."

"Twenty thousand?"

"Above and beyond your fee, of course," she added. "It's a bonus."

She obviously learned from her husbands.

"Never mind a bonus," I said. "I want half the twenty thousand up front."

She smiled, reached into her purse, came out with a brown envelope and slid it across the table at me.

"I thought you might," she said. "Also in there is all the information you'll need—where you can find my husband and me, where his daughters live with their husbands, where they work. Everything I could think of. And my phone number and address, in case you have any other questions."

"Don't worry, I will," I said, pocketing the envelope.

"Do you have any questions now?"

"Yeah, I do," I said. "What makes you think somebody's trying to kill him?"

"Accidents,'" she said. "The brakes gave out on one of his cars. It was only the expert driving of the chauffer that kept them from crashing. Then a live wire found its way into our Jacuzzi. He almost got in before he spotted it."

"That would've been shocking," I said. "What did your husband say about it?"

"That a loose wire is an accident," she said. "And bad brakes could happen to anybody."

"But you don't believe it."

"No," she said, "not the Jacuzzi and not the brakes."

"Where do you live when you're not in New York?" I asked.

"We have a house in Maine, a villa in France, an estate in Carmel."

That sounded like it'd be a lot of traveling for me to check out all three.

"Where's the Jacuzzi?"

"In Maine."

"And where'd the trouble with the brakes happen?"

"In France."

Back in the day I would've sent some of my ops to check those places out.

"Anything else?"

"Yes," she said, "somebody took a shot at him."

"Where?"

"Upstate New York."

"How did he write that off as an accident?"

"He was hunting, at the time," she said. "He said it was a stray shot."

"Did it hit him?"

"No, but it came close."

"And you're sure it was deliberate?"

"Look, Johnny," she said, "even if I'm wrong, I've got to know that, too. And it's worth twenty thousand to me. Now, do you have any more questions?"

I had to admit, she was either very concerned, or she'd gotten even better over the years at playing me, because she was doing this without sex.

Yeah, I did, but the question was for me. Why the hell wasn't I just getting up and walking out?

"Yeah, as a matter of fact, I do," I said. "Where the hell is my coffee cantata?"

EIGHT

Fool me once, shame on me.

Fool me twice, and I deserve whatever the hell I get.

I left Keens with my stomach full and, soon, my bank account, too. Was any of that worth giving Carla/Constance the chance to screw me, again? I figured I should probably go back to Tenth Avenue and let those three guys kick my ass again, first.

But twenty grand is twenty grand and Constance Pennyworth was right about one thing. I had been struggling since I got out of prison.

"You what?" Ally asked, when I got back to the office.

"I agreed to work for the woman who sent me to jail," I repeated.

She folded her arms and said, "You're gonna have to explain that one to me."

"Let's go someplace and get a drink," I suggested.

There was a bar we sometimes hit after work. A lot of other people did the same thing, so we elbowed ourselves two spots at the bar. But most of the afterwork crowd hit the bar at five when they left the office, and headed home around six. We got there at seven, because Ally had been waiting for me to get back. We were able to talk without having to shout, and I gave her the story of the time of my life I tended to think of as Headstone's Folly.

"Jesus," she said, when I was done, "so that's why you have twelve empty desks"

"Pretty much."

We simplified the drinking by ordering bottled beer, so I waved to the bartender for two more Fat Tires.

"But what I don't understand," she said, "is why, when you saw who it was, you didn't turn around and walk out."

"Well," I said, "it was Keens."

"Steak? How much better can it be than the Outback?"

I stared at her.

"Okay, so steak, and...?"

"Twenty thousand dollars."

She whistled, making several heads turn.

"So she wants to give you twenty grand to make up for sendin' you to jail?"

"Not quite," I said. "It's a job."

"You took a job from the old girlfriend who played you for a sap?" she asked.

"That's about the size of it."

"Why not turn her over to the police?"

"They don't want her," I said. "They have the guy who killed her husband."

"And now?"

"Somebody wants to kill her new husband."

"A rich husband?"

"Oh, yeah."

"Does he knows she's givin' you twenty thousand of his money?" she asked.

"Probably not."

"Are you sure she's not hirin' you to kill 'im?"

"She doesn't want him dead," I said. "She hasn't gotten him

to change his will, yet."

"Ah," she said, "so who wants him dead?"

"That's what she wants me to find out," I said, "but she thinks it's one of his daughters."

"Oh God, his own daughters?" she asked. "That's crazy."

"Well," I said, "Carl—Constance figures the daughters don't want him to change his will, and at least one of them—or their husbands—are willing to kill him to keep him from doin' it."

"I guess that makes sense," she commented. "Let me ask you one thing, though."

"What's that?"

"Are you over this broad?"

"Hey, Ally," I said, "I got over that broad while I was in Sing Sing."

"You were in Sing Sing?" she said, raising her eyebrows. "That place is famous. What was it like?"

"It was just like bein' in prison."

We left the bar and she said, "Are you going home to your new place?"

I had moved into a new apartment a couple of weeks earlier. I needed a cheaper place, so got a one bedroom in an East Village basement.

"Yeah," I said. "I've still got decorating to do."

"You want some help?"

"Go home," I said, "have dinner, go to bed early. Tomorrow we start work."

"I'm gonna work with you on this?"

"I'm payin' you, ain't I?"

"Sometimes."

"Well," I said, "I will, this time."

I remembered that I had an envelope in my jacket pocket with ten grand in it. I'd have to hit the bank in the morning.

"I owe you two weeks back pay," I told her. "You'll have it

tomorrow."

"That suits me," she said, happily. "I'll see you in the morning."

NINE

My new apartment in the East Village was a basement hole. That was why I didn't want Ally to come and help me "decorate." After two weeks I was already arguing with my landlord about the standing water in the shower. It usually took all day to drain away. He promised to have a look at it, but hadn't yet. I was thinking about calling a plumber myself, but they charged an arm-and-a-leg. However, now that I had the Pennyworth ten grand, I decided to make the call.

I stopped in a small market on the way home, picked up a can of coffee and a Sara Lee pound cake. I was still full from the meal at Keens, but I knew that later on I'd want something.

There was a dumpster on my block, so I stopped and got rid of my torn jacket and pants. I was thinking about getting some new duds with the ten grand, but decided I'd better bank it and catch up on Ally's salary before I did any more. A plumber, coffee and cake would have to do, for a while.

When I got home I sat at the small desk in my office, which for anyone else would have been a dining area. I needed the office, so I usually took my meals on the coffee table in front of the TV, and gave up the idea of a dining room table and chairs set-up.

Carla—it was still hard for me to think of her as "Constance"—had done a good job filling me in on the Pennyworth family.

Her husband was in shipping and real estate, had inherited money from his father and grandfather, but had managed to triple the fortune on his own. He wasn't in *Forbes'* top fifty, but he was close.

The daughters were both in their thirties, both lived on the east coast, one in Manhattan and the other in Vermont.

The older daughter, Angela, was married to Harrison Wayne, a stockbroker, which explained why they chose to live in Manhattan. The younger daughter—Sarah, thirty-two, three years the younger—was married to her second husband, a Brit named Piers Rohmer who was an "entrepreneur," which probably meant he was a gambler. She had divorced her first husband after three years for "irreconcilable differences."

I looked through the file folder and found that Constance Pennyworth had resisted making notes with her own opinions. I assumed she was expecting me to question the daughters, but I didn't know if she expected me to talk to her husband. She certainly hadn't warned me away from him.

I checked the time, saw that it was nine p.m. I didn't expect she'd be asleep yet, but if she was, too bad. One if the last things she'd told me before I left Keens was that she and her husband were staying at the Four Seasons. I guessed if Alan had been in the *Forbes'* top fifty they'd be at the Plaza.

"Hello?"

"Mrs. Pennyworth," I said.

"Johnny?" she lowered her voice. "Have you found out something, already?"

"No," I said, "I just had a question for you."

"What is it?"

"Do you expect me to have a talk with your husband about any of this?"

"I suppose—but can't you investigate without doing that, Johnny?" she asked.

"I don't think so," I said. "I need to know what he thinks is going on."

She sighed heavily into the phone and said, "Oh, all right."

"What did you tell him about me?"

"That you were recommended by a friend."

"Does the friend have a name?"

"He didn't ask."

"All right, then," I said. "Will I find him at the Four Seasons tomorrow?"

"In the morning, yes," she said, "but he's got meetings in the afternoon."

"Okay," I said, "I'll make sure I get there early."

"I'll be there." It sounded like a promise.

"That's probably not a good idea," I said. "Go shopping, or get your hair done."

"Like a good little wifey?"

"Exactly."

"Yeah, okay," she said, and hung up.

She seemed offended. At least, I hoped so.

I hung up and hit the hay. Happily, I didn't dream about Carla Balducci. I hoped I never would again.

TEN

I hit the bank first in the morning, deposited most of the money, then picked up bagels and coffee before going to the office. As the old elevator slowly made its way up, the interior filled with the scent of breakfast.

I walked in and held the bags up on display.

"Finally," Ally said. "I'm starving."

"Sorry," I said, setting the bags down on her desk. "I had to stop at the bank for this." I took out an envelope and set it down in front of her. "Back pay, plus."

"Oooh, plus?" she asked, picking it up with a smile.

"Overtime."

"Thank you." She tucked it away in a pocket.

"You can count it," I said.

"Tacky," she said. "I'll wait until I'm alone." She grabbed the bag of bagels, fished hers out, and handed the rest to me. I took it into my office with the coffee, sat at my desk.

"No messages?" I called out.

"Not this early."

"Good."

Who would've called, anyway, except for Constance, or maybe Steve Ryder?

I ate two bagels—a poppy seed and a sesame seed, both with butter—and drank my coffee, then went back out.

"I'm going to the Four Seasons," I said. "Be back later."

"You goin' for a little nooner?" she asked.

"I'm going to talk with Alan Pennyworth about who's tryin' to kill him."

"Well, that's all right, then."

"Besides," I said, on my way out the door, "it's way too early for a nooner."

Constance had given me the room number, so there was no need for me to stop at the desk. They would have just looked at me like I didn't belong.

When I knocked, the door was opened by a tall, grey-haired gent in a suit and shoes I would've bet were Italian, except I didn't know enough to actually identify those things. Let's just say they looked expensive.

"Mr. Pennyworth?"

"Mr. Headston, I presume," he said, pronouncing my name correctly.

"Your wife told you I was comin'?"

"Yes." He backed away. "Come in."

I expected him to have a suite, but instead it was one of the Four Seasons' regular rooms. Still, compared to most hotels, it was a palace.

Pennyworth stopped in the center of the room and turned to face me.

"Can I offer you something?" he asked. "Coffee? Juice?"

"No, thanks," I said. "I just need a few minutes of your time."

"Look," he said, "I know my wife hired you, but she's got a vivid imagination."

"She told me about failed brakes, a hot wire in the Jacuzzi, and a close shot during a hunting trip. Are all those things true?"

"Well...yes."

"Then maybe we can sit down and talk?"

His thin shoulders slumped.

"Have a seat," he said.

He was wearing a grey suit with a lavender shirt that looked like silk, all dressed for whatever important meetings he had planned for later in the day. His complexion was as grey as his suit, the skin of his face wrinkled and dry. His eyebrows were tufts of gray that made him look perpetually surprised. He would've looked better shaving them off.

"What do you want to know?" he asked. I noticed his teeth had a yellowish tint, probably from years of smoking.

"Who wants to kill you?"

"Nobody."

"Who would have a motive to kill you?"

"Business associates."

"Rivals?"

He shrugged.

"I'm too old and tired to be very interested in such things as rivalries."

"Too old and tired to deal with somebody tryin' to kill you?" I asked.

He leaned forward.

"How much is my wife paying you?"

"My usual fee," I said, "plus expenses. I'll bill her when it's all over."

"And do you know my wife?"

"I met Mrs. Pennyworth yesterday, at Keens."

"Not before?"

"No."

I wasn't lying to him. When I first met her, she wasn't Mrs. Pennyworth.

"So what now?" Pennyworth asked.

"What about your daughters and their husbands?"

"What about them?" Suddenly, he looked shocked. "Wait, did Constance tell you that they—"

"No, no," I said, "I'm just asking about them...how do they

feel about you marrying Constance?"

"We've been married twelve years," he said. "My daughters and I discussed it then. We don't talk about it anymore."

"What about your will?"

"What about it?"

"Is Constance in it?"

"Of course."

"Then my question is, how do your daughters and their husbands feel about that?"

"I haven't discussed it with them."

"They haven't made their feelings known?"

"No."

"In most families that wouldn't be the case."

"Is that a fact?" he asked.

"Yes, it is," I said. "I've dealt with these situations before. The children never like it when their rich fathers take a young bride."

"Constance is not that much younger," Pennyworth said.

"Twenty years, isn't it?"

"It may be," Pennyworth said, "but I didn't marry her to have a trophy wife. I love her."

"I'm going to talk with your daughters," I told him.

"Don't you accuse them of anything!" he snapped.

"Then do us both a favor," I said.

"What?"

"Tell me what you think of your sons-in-law?"

He studied me for a few seconds, then said, "Fine. Angela's husband Harrison is a waste, and Sarah's husband Piers is even worse. Happy?"

"So if you don't like them, they probably don't like you," I said. "Were they with you when you were hunting?"

He paused, then said, "Yes."

"You may not think your daughters would try to kill you, but what about Harrison and Piers?"

He thought it over.

"I wouldn't have thought they'd have the guts," he said, finally.

"Are you willing to admit one or both of them might be behind the attempts?"

"It's possible," he relented.

"Okay," I said. "Let's talk."

ELEVEN

Pennyworth either couldn't, or didn't want to, come up with any other names as suspects.

"Then tell me," I said, "who could?"

"Excuse me?"

"Who should I talk to who could give me some names?" I asked. "I mean, other than your wife?"

"No one."

"Don't you have a...a chief of staff, or a manager, or someone working for you who I could talk to?"

"No," Pennyworth said, "I handle my own affairs."

I didn't argue with him, because I knew somebody who'd be able to fill me in. But for now, my suspect list was all family.

"All right," I said, standing.

"Is that it?" he asked, also standing. "You're done? You'll bill Constance?"

"I'm not anywhere near finished, Mr. Pennyworth," I said. "I'm just finished talkin' to you."

"So you're going after my family?" he asked. "My daughters?"

"I'm not going after anyone, sir," I said. "I'll just do my job and see what happens."

He walked me to the door.

"I must warn you I'm going to have a talk with Constance to try to get her to terminate your services. If she does, I'll make sure you're compensated."

"Whatever the two of you decide," I said. "Until I hear different, I'm going to continue to do my job."

He didn't comment further, simply closed the door behind me so quickly it almost hit me in the butt.

I had a friend who used to be a stockbroker. He burned out on the job, and now he's homeless—except for a bench in Bryant Park, located on Sixth Avenue behind the New York Public Library main branch. The park was actually built on top of an underground space that houses the library's stacks. Although it's a public park, it's managed by the Bryant Park Corporation.

As usual I saw Jack was sitting on his bench, reading the financial pages of the *Wall Street Journal* rather than staring out at the expanse of well-manicured lawn in front of him. He was never dressed like a homeless person. He was usually clean, and always sober. And he was always available to hand out advice and stock tips to people who knew enough to stop by and ask. All he asked in return was a donation, usually cash, sometimes food or drink.

"Hey Jack," I said, approaching and bearing gifts.

"I smell coffee," he said.

I handed him the bag I was carrying. Inside was a container of coffee, a plain bagel slathered with butter, and a twenty-dollar bill. I also handed him the current issues of *Barron's* and *The Economist*, two financial magazines I knew he ordered.

"Thanks, Johnny," he said. The twenty went into a pocket, the coffee on the bench next to him on the left, the magazines on the right, and he unwrapped the bagel and took a bite. "How can I help?"

I sat with the container of coffee between us.

"Alan Pennyworth."

"Rich man," Jack said, "but not disgustingly so."

He not only had a limitless knowledge of stocks, but also

anything that had to do with high finance.

"Who'd want to kill 'im, Jack?"

He stopped chewing and stared at me, then slowly started chewing again as he considered the question.

"What about family members?" he asked. "I mean, he does have a younger bride."

"As he pointed out to me, not so young," I said.

"Well, yeah, she'd be over fifty, but he's over seventy. It's all relative, ain't it?" He pried the lid off the coffee container and took a sip. I'd gotten it hot and black, the way he liked it.

"I'm workin' on family, already," I said. "I need your opinion when it comes to his business dealings."

"The gent's kinda odd," Jack said.

"In what way?"

"Most moguls have money managers," he said. "This guy handles all his own business."

"So he's smart."

"Very."

"Then how would he get taken by a money hungry whore?" I asked.

Jack paused with his coffee halfway to his mouth and looked at me.

"This sounds like somebody you know."

"Once."

"Well," Jack said, "maybe they're in love."

"Right," I said. "She married him for his money, and is tryin' to get him to change his will, leaving her everything. That's love."

"He has two daughters," Jack said. "You suspect them?"

"They're on my list," I said. "What I was hoping to get from you was another list."

"Of business rivals."

"Yes."

"What about people within his own businesses?"

"That, too, if there are any."

"Well," Jack said, "I'll need some time."

"Can I have it by tomorrow?"

"You don't ask for much."

"Pastrami?" I asked.

"On a hoagie, not on rye?" Jack asked.

"You got it."

"Then so do you."

"Tomorrow, lunch is on me," I said.

TWELVE

Angela and Harrison Wayne lived in a high rise on the upper
West side. I took the subway, came up on Amsterdam Avenue.
Only when I was a block from their building did I take out my
cell phone and call the number Constance had given me in her
file.

"Hello?" a woman said.

"Angela?"

"Who's this?"

"My name is John Headston, I'm a private investigator. I'm
looking into attempts on your father's life."

"What? Who is th—who hired you? What attempts?"

"Were you on a hunting trip with him when he almost got
shot?" I asked.

"My husband was."

"Well," I said, "that was one."

"That was an accident—wait, there were other attempts?"

"Yes."

"When?"

"I'd like to come up and talk to you and your husband about
it."

"Do you know where we live?"

"I'm a block away," I told her.

"Come on up, then. There's no doorman. We're in nineteen-A."

51

She hung up.

I put my phone back in my pocket and walked the rest of the way to their building, which was right across the street from Central Park.

I took the elevator to the nineteenth floor, walked to apartment A and knocked. The woman who answered was tall and thin, much like her father, but there the resemblance ended. She must have looked more like her mother in the face, which was lucky for her. She was attractive, but a lot of it had to do with the proper use of make-up. She had a mass of red hair that fell in waves to her shoulders. It was the perfect color to go with her knee-length green dress.

"Mr. Headston?"

"That's right."

"I'm sorry," she said. "Do you have ID?"

"Of course." I showed her both my driver's and my PI licenses.

"Come in, please."

She backed away to allow me to come in, then closed the door and waved.

"In there," she said.

I walked ahead of her into a large living room with a window overlooking the park.

"Is your husband joining us?"

"Harrison is not home right now," she said. "It's just you and me. Have a seat." She waved at an expensive sofa. "Would you like a drink? Perhaps some coffee?"

"A cup of coffee would be fine."

"I'll be back."

I'd expected her to have someone do that for her, but she left and came back with a tray. She set it down on the coffee table, then sat across from me.

"Cream and sugar?" she asked.

"Just black, thanks."

She handed me a mug of coffee, then sat back. There was another mug on the tray, but she didn't fill it. I noticed her arms were very well-toned.

"How can I help?" she asked.

"On the phone you didn't sound like you believed someone was trying to kill your father."

"I had to think about it a minute," she admitted. "The brakes in his car? The Jacuzzi? The stray shot during the hunting trip. They can't all be accidents."

"No," I said, "they can't. So who do you think has a reason to kill him?"

"A business rival?"

"Do you have one in mind?"

"I don't know his dealings well enough to say," she said. "What about Constance?"

"She's actually the one who hired me," I said, "but that doesn't eliminate her from consideration. I'm looking at everybody. I assume that's what you were asking?"

"Yes. And I'm glad to hear it," she said.

"You think she wants him dead?"

"I used to think so."

"What changed?" I asked.

"Twelve years," Angela said. "If she wanted him dead, he probably would've been long before this."

"Makes sense."

"What was her best guess?" Angela asked.

"Well—"

"Let me think," she said, cutting me off. "Me or my sister? To keep her out of the will?"

"She, uh, did mention that as a possibility."

"I haven't tried to kill my father, Mr. Headston," she told me, "but I can't speak for my sister, Sarah. You'd have to ask her yourself."

"I plan to," I responded, "but I also want to talk to your husbands."

"Our husbands," Angela repeated, thoughtfully. "Is that what Constance said? That she thinks one of our husbands might be doing it?"

"I thought I told you," I commented, "everyone's under consideration."

We both heard the front door open at that point, and then slam closed.

"Angie?" a man's voice called. "I'm back."

She smiled at me.

"You said you wanted to talk to my husband," she said, starting to get to her feet. "Now's your chance."

THIRTEEN

She intercepted her husband before he came into the living room. I heard a muffled conversation, and then they both came walking in. I was surprised to find that the near six feet Angela was married to about five feet eight of Harrison. He was wearing an expensive suit, and a purple silk shirt with no tie.

"Mr....Headston, is it?" he asked.

"That's right." I stood.

He extended his hand and I shook it. A Rolex gleamed on his wrist.

"Do you mind?" he asked, pointing to the empty coffee mug.

"Not at all."

"Sit, please."

He sat in the chair his wife had been in moments before, poured himself some coffee. She sat on the arm of the chair, leaning on his shoulder.

He sipped his coffee, set the mug down.

"My wife says you're investigating attempts on my father-in-law's life."

"She's correct."

"She also says you suspect me."

"I suspect everyone, at the moment."

"Even that bitch he's married to?"

"Even her."

He was not only shorter than his wife, but if I was right, he was about five years younger.

"Well," Harrison Wayne said, "it wasn't me. Or my wife."

"How well do you know your brother-in-law?"

"Not well at all," Wayne said. "Fact is, I don't like him. I preferred Sarah's first husband."

Angela made a rude noise.

Wayne smiled.

"My wife hated him, but he was a fun guy."

"He was an asshole," Angela said. "He cheated on my sister and hurt her."

"Well, your sister is kind of a bitch."

"Harrison!"

Wayne looked at me and winked. I hated him.

I stood.

"Well, I guess that's it," I said. "If either of you can think of someone I should look into, I'd appreciate a call." I put my card down on the coffee tray.

"Headstone Detective Agency," Wayne read. "I get it."

"I'll walk you out," Angela said.

She accompanied me to the front door. When she turned to face me we were eye to eye. Hers were green. I was willing to bet mine were bloodshot.

"Thanks for your time," I said.

"Thank you for what you're doing," she responded.

"It's my job."

"Nevertheless…" She reached out and touched my arm.

In the hall, with the door between us, I could still feel her touch.

"What's she like?" Ally asked, when I got back to the office. "The daughter."

"Classy."

"And the husband?"

"Short."

"What?"

"Well," I said, "shorter than her. I'll bet in her stocking feet she's still nearly six feet tall. Takes after her father in that way."

"Attractive?" Ally asked.

"Very."

"Johnny…" Her tone was a warning.

"Relax," I said, "I told you she's married."

"Yeah, to a short guy."

"Shorter than me, yes," I said, "but younger and better lookin'. No worries there, Ally."

"I hope not. You've got enough trouble working for an old girlfriend—"

"Not a girlfriend," I said, cutting her off.

"Well, whatever you wanna call 'er," she said. "She's trouble, and you don't need more."

"My days of women trouble are over, Ally."

"Ha!" she said. "No man's days of women trouble are ever over."

I ignored the comment and went into my office. I'd interviewed father, daughter and son-in-law with no great revelations coming to light. The other daughter, Sarah, and her husband lived in Vermont, and to interview them I'd either have to fly there, or do it by phone. I hated the idea of not doing it in person. You lost so much when all you have to go on is a voice, and you can't see facial expressions. I was going to have to make up my mind pretty soon.

But I didn't want to leave town before I saw Jack the next afternoon. I wanted to hear what he had to say about Alan Pennyworth's financial enemies.

I spent the rest of the day doing some paperwork, catching up on how many more services I had to do that week.

Once I finished serving the rest of the papers for Steve Ryder, I'd be free to concentrate on the Pennyworth case, which included a possible trip to Vermont.

"I'm goin' home," Ally said, from the door. "You need anythin' else from me?"

"No, go ahead," I said. "I'll be here a little while longer. See you in the morning."

"Good-night, Johnny," she said. "Don't do anythin' I wouldn't."

"Go!" I said.

About an hour later I was getting ready to leave when the phone rang.

"Headstone Agency," I said.

"Johnny? It's...Constance."

She paused before saying her name. Had she been confused in that moment about whether she was Carla or not?

"I've got nothin' to report, Constance," I said. "I talked with your husband. Also spoke to Angela and her husband, but I haven't come to any—"

"I'm not calling about that," she said. "I just...wanted to talk to you."

She was slurring her words a bit, so I assumed she'd had a few.

"Talk about what?"

"Us," she said, and I thought I heard ice tinkle in a glass. "Do you ever think about us?"

"No, I don't," I said. "If I ever think about you, Carla, it reminds me of what a fool I was."

"Oh, Johnny..." she said. She didn't seem to have anything to add after that.

"Stop drinking, Constance," I said, "and get some sleep. Cuddle up to your husband."

"We don't sleep in the same bedroom," she said.

"That's not something I'm interested in hearin'," I told her. "Good-night, Constance. I'll call you when I have somethin' to report."

"Johnny—" she started, but I hung up.

When I went to sleep that night I didn't dream about Constance Pennyworth. Instead, I dreamed about Angela Wayne.

FOURTEEN

I woke the next morning, still sore from the kicking I'd gotten on Tenth Avenue. I decided to have breakfast in, so I made a pot of coffee and had two cups with a bowl of cereal.

On the way to the office, though, I still stopped for coffee and bagels for Ally. And I figured I might as well include one of each for myself. You don't get a bulging fifty-year-old waistline without trying.

When I got to the office Ally was busy on her computer. She usually brought her laptop from home with her, and she convinced me to buy a new one for my office. As I put the bagel bag on her desk she held up one hand without looking up from her screen. It held a bouquet of pink message slips.

"The phone's been ringing all mornin'," she told me.

"All these messages came in this morning?" I asked. "I haven't had these many in years."

"Don't get all excited." She finally looked up from her screen, grabbed the bag and reached in for one. "They're all from the same person."

"Oh? Who?" I hadn't looked yet, so I was afraid it was Constance.

"Sarah Rohmer?" she said, taking the top off her coffee. "Do you know her?"

"Yeah," I said, "that's Alan Pennyworth's other daughter."

"Well, she sounded pretty frantic, so you better call her back."

"I'll do that now," I said.

I went into my office, put my bagel and coffee down on my desk and looked at the messages. Then I went back out to Ally.

"Is this a Vermont area code?" I asked.

"No, but that doesn't really matter," she said. "Remember, with cell phones the area code you need to call is usually the one where the phone was purchased."

"Right."

I went back into my office, sat at my desk and used my cell phone to return the call, rather than my business landline, which Ally kept saying I should get rid of.

"Hello, this is John Headston returning Sarah Rohmer's calls."

"Mr. Headston," she said, "this is Sarah Pennyworth. I never took my husband's name."

"That's fine," I said. "Do I call you Miss Pennyworth, Mrs. Pennyworth, Mrs. Rohmer...what?"

"Just Sarah," she said. "I have to see you."

"I've been thinkin' about comin' up to Vermont—"

"I'm here," she said, "In New York."

"With your husband? Because I'd like to talk to him, too."

"That's what I need to discuss with you," she said. "My husband."

"Why? What about him?"

"He's trying to kill me."

I had to meet with Jack for lunch first, so I arranged to see Sarah right after that. In fact, I told her to meet me at Bryant Park.

"That's good," she said. "It'll be out in the open."

"And then we can find a place to talk."

When I put my phone down I looked up and saw Ally standing at the door.

"What's she so fired up about?" she asked.

"She says her husband's tryin' to kill 'er."

"Really?" Ally said. "So, does that mean he's also tryin' to kill her father?"

"I don't know, Ally," I said. "This might be two separate things."

"Oh dude, that'd be one helluva coincidence, wouldn't it?" she asked.

"Yeah, it would."

"Want me to meet 'er?" she asked. "Keep 'er company while you meet with your buddy?"

"No," I said, "but I might need you later, if this does turn out to be two separate things."

"Cool," she said. "I can use some time out of the office."

"We'll see."

"I got one question, though."

"What's that?"

"When do I get a gun?"

FIFTEEN

I picked up Jack's pastrami sandwich at the Times Deli, on West Forty-Fifth Street. In fact I got two, one for each of us, with fries and a pickle. I also picked up three bottles of Dr. Brown's Cream Soda, one for me, and two for Jack. It was carried in all the Jewish delis in New York, and sported the slogan "Imported from the old neighborhood."

"Right on time," Jack said, as I approached his bench. He set aside his newspaper and rubbed his hands together.

I sat down next to him and handed him his bag. I'd had the cashier bag our food separately.

"Yes," he said, reverently, as he unwrapped it and took a bite. Then he looked into the bag again. "Dr. Brown's?"

"What else?"

He put the sandwich down, took the soda out and popped it open. After one sip he rolled his eyes.

"So okay," I said, unwrapping my own sandwich., "What've you got for me?"

"Your guy's got an endless supply of enemies," Jack said. "He makes a habit of buying up failing companies, and then instead of trying to prop them up, he loots them."

"And people lose their jobs."

"Lots of people," he said, "and lots of jobs. From janitors to the CEO, they'd all like to kill him. I hope that helps." He grinned with a mouthful of pastrami.

"Actually," I said, "it doesn't help at all."

I was still leaning toward family. Anyone could have tampered with the brakes, or hotwired his Jacuzzi, but he was hunting with his family. I had to look further into that little outing.

Sarah Pennyworth was waiting for me at the gate when I left Bryant Park. She was tall and slender, like her father and sister, but in her case it was painfully so. Her cheekbones stood out like they were going to poke through her face. She was wearing a jacket that did nothing to hide the sharpness of her collarbone and elbows. She needed to put on twenty pounds or more just to look healthy.

"Friend of yours?" she asked, looking over at Jack.

"One of my operatives," I said. "Working undercover."

"Ah." She looked around nervously.

"Come on," I said, "let's walk."

"I'm afraid I'm being followed," she said, as we started.

"By who?"

"I don't know."

"Your husband?"

"Maybe somebody he hired."

"To kill you?"

She hunched her shoulders and shuddered, as if cold.

"Okay," I said, "we're going to have to sit down and discuss all of this."

"Where?"

"Are you hungry?"

"No."

"Well," I said, "you look like you could eat. Come on."

I walked her over to Eighth Avenue to a diner I sometimes ate at. I hadn't finished my pastrami sandwich, leaving it with Jack so he could eat it later. I also let him finish my Dr. Brown's. So even though she still insisted she wasn't hungry, I ordered a burger platter for both of us. As soon as they came she started to eat the french fries.

"First," I said, "I wanted to talk to you about somebody tryin' to kill your father."

"I heard about that from my sister, Angela."

I studied her. Unlike Angela's red hair, Sarah had gone blond. But she still had the freckles of a redhead across the bridge of her nose.

"She gave me your number," she added.

"Do you know of anyone who'd want to kill your father?"

She shrugged and said, "Anybody who does business with him, I guess."

"What about this hunting trip he was on, where he was almost shot?"

"What about it?"

"Who was with him?"

"My husband, and Angela's."

"That's it? No business partners?"

"My father doesn't have business partners," she said. "You either work for him, or he grinds you under his heel."

"Well then," I said, "if he was almost shot, it was one of the husbands. If you think yours is tryin' to kill you, do you think he's also after your father?"

"No," she said, "I don't think one has to do with the other."

"Why not?"

"My husband just wants to get rid of me."

"Before you inherit?"

"I don't think he can wait that long," she said. "He'll take what he can get now."

"Your father's gettin' up there."

"It wouldn't surprise me if my father outlived both Angela and me," she said. "He's healthy as a horse."

"He looks pretty frail, to me."

"Well, he's not," she said. "Take my word for it."

"All right, then," I said, "Tell me why you think your husband wants to kill you."

"I put that wrong," she said. "He's not trying to kill me. He's going to have me killed. Somebody already tampered with the brakes on my car. And when that didn't work I was almost run down in the street."

"Why?"

"Why do husbands want to get rid of wives?" she asked. "I guess he's tired of me."

"Is there somebody else?"

She picked up a fry, dipped it in some ketchup, and popped it into her mouth. She still hadn't touched the burger. "I don't know. Maybe. Piers was a ladies man when I met him."

"What do you want me to do, Sarah?"

"I want you to keep Piers from killing me."

"Don't you want me to prove whether he actually is tryin' to kill you?"

"Who else could it be?"

I was of the opposite opinion. If someone was trying to kill the father, and the daughter, it had to be connected. Especially since both of them had their brakes tampered with.

"Where are you staying?" I asked.

"With my sister."

"Good, I'll take you over there, I want to talk to Angela."

If somebody was trying to kill Sarah and her father, then why not Angela, too? Maybe somebody was after the entire Pennyworth family.

I started to get up.

"Wait," she said.

"For what?"

"You said I should eat." She picked up the hamburger. "Suddenly, I'm hungry."

I'd been eating all along, and my plate was empty. I sat back down to wait.

SIXTEEN

When Angela opened the door to let us in Sarah grabbed her and the two sisters hugged.

"Is your husband home?" I asked.

"No," she said, "he's at work."

"We should talk."

"Then you better come in."

I followed them to the living room.

"Sit there," she told her sister, depositing her on the sofa, "I'll get you a drink." She looked at me and nodded toward a chair.

"Make mine bourbon," I said.

She left the room and came back with a drink for me and Sarah. Nothing for herself.

"Did she tell you?" Angela asked.

"She did. She thinks her husband wants her dead."

"Well, that makes us even," Angela said. "I'd like to see him dead. We told her not to marry him." She sat next to Sarah and put her arm around her, protectively. "What can you do?"

"Just what I'm doin'," I said. "What Constance hired me to do."

"That bitch!" Sarah snapped.

"That may be," I said, "but she doesn't want your father to be killed."

"So she says," Angela replied. "How do we know she's not behind the attempts on his life?"

"If she is, why hire me?" I asked.

Angela hesitated, then said, "I don't know."

"Look, both of you, this has to be connected. The brakes on your father's and Sarah's car failing can't be a coincidence."

"Then if someone is trying to kill father and Sarah," Angela said, "why not me?"

"That's what I came here to ask you, Angela," I said. "What aren't you tellin' me?"

"I was in the subway a while back," she said, "on the platform waiting for the Grand Central shuttle. I was shoved from behind and fell onto the tracks. Because it was the shuttle, there was time for people to help me back up before the train came."

"Did you see who pushed you?"

"No. By the time I got back onto the platform, they were gone."

"Did you tell anyone?"

"Only my husband."

"What did he say?"

"That I was imagining things."

"Then she told me," Sarah said, "and I told her about my close calls. But I think hers could've been an accident."

"It could've been," Angela said, to me, "but what are the chances that all of this is coincidence?"

"None," I said. "Somebody's trying to kill your whole family."

"But not our husbands," Angela said. "Just the two of us and our father. Why?"

"That's what I'm gonna try to find out," I said.

Angela removed her arm from her sister's shoulders and stood up to face me.

"We'll hire you," she said, "Sarah and I."

"I already have a client."

"Well, I'm not convinced that client has our best interests at heart."

"What's the difference?" I asked. "The result will be the same. I'll find out who's behind all of this."

"Is there any law that says you can't have more than one client?" Sarah asked.

"Well, no, but—" I started, but Angela cut me off.

"Then I'll write you a check," she said. "It'll be up to you if you cash it."

She walked to a small writing desk in a corner of the room, sat down, took a checkbook from the drawer and wrote a check. She tore it off and carried it over to me.

"This should be sufficient for now."

I took it and looked at it. She'd written it for five thousand.

"As you say," I told her, pocketing it, "I'll decide later whether I'm gonna cash it or not."

"All right, then," she said, sitting next to her sister again, "so what do we do now?"

"You go someplace safe," I said, "and only I'll know where you are."

"Not our husbands?" Angela asked.

"Do you trust your husband?" I asked.

"I don't know that I trust him," she said, "but I don't think he's trying to kill me."

"Well, your sister does think her husband's tryin' to kill her," I said. "And if he is, he might be behind the attempts on you and your father, as well. I'd rather nobody but me knows where you are."

"My father won't go for that," Angela said.

"I'm worried about you two," I said. "Once I'm convinced you're safe, I can concentrate on your father. I find who's tryin' to kill him, and I think I'll find out who's behind the whole mess. Is there somewhere you can go?"

"Not somewhere my husband wouldn't know about," she said. "Would you have a place?"

"I might be able to find one," I said. "But right now I'll take the two of you to my office. You can stay there until I figure something out."

"I'll get my things," Angela said, leaving her sister on the sofa.

"How well do you know my sister?" Sarah asked.

"About as well as I know you," I said.

"And Constance?"

I hesitated, then said, "A little better."

"My sister thinks you know what you're doing. At least, that's what she told me when she called."

"I like to think so," I said, but I didn't add that it hadn't always been the case.

SEVENTEEN

When we got to the office Ally was still there, so I made the introductions.

"Can I get you something?" Ally asked.

"No, we're fine."

"Go on into my office," I told them.

As they went through Ally said to me, "I didn't want to close the office until you got back. What are they doin' here?"

"It seems Alan may not be the only Pennyworth who's in danger," I said.

"Them too?" she asked. "Somebody's tryin' to kill the whole family?"

"That's the way it seems."

"What are you gonna do with them?"

"I need to find a safe place to put them," I said.

"Like where?"

I shrugged. "I'm still thinking."

"How about my place?"

I had never been to Ally's place, so I didn't know how big it was.

"Do you have enough room for three women?" I asked.

She smiled.

"It's big enough" she said, "thanks to Daddy paying my rent."

I'd never known that, either.

"I have a loft in the West Village," she said. "Eighteen hundred square feet."

I hesitated.

"What's the matter? Don't trust me?"

"I don't want to put you in danger," I said, "if there is somebody tryin' to kill them."

"You've used me a time or two before and I've done okay, haven't I?"

"You've done great."

"And nobody's gonna know they're with me," she said. "We should be safe."

"Okay, Ally." I said. "I'll tell 'em."

"Besides," she added, "I get a gun, right?"

"We'll talk about that."

She frowned.

"That's what you always say."

The sisters went for it when I presented it to them.

"Nobody will know you're there, and Ally says she has plenty of room."

"We should stop for some food on the way, though," Ally said. "I eat out and get delivery a lot."

"A good Chinese take-out?" Sarah asked.

"The best," Ally assured her.

"Sounds good," Angela said.

"I'll close up," Ally said, leaving my office.

"What are you going to be doing while we're hiding and eating Chinese food?" Angela asked.

"I'm gonna talk to Constance, again," I said. "Maybe she knows more than she's telling me."

"No Uber?" Angela asked, as I waved down a yellow cab.

"I'm old fashioned."

We let the three ladies out in front of Ally's place.

"When will you be back?" Sarah asked.

"Probably a couple of hours."

"We'll order enough food for you, too," Ally promised.

"Thanks."

I watched them go in, then told the driver to take me to Constance Pennyworth's hotel.

"Johnny," she said, when she opened her door. "I wasn't expecting you."

"I know," I said, "that's why I didn't call. Is your husband here?"

"No," she said, "he has meetings today."

"Good," I said. "We need to talk."

She was dressed to go out, wearing a tight-fitting grey jacket, a skirt that barely came to the knees of her toned legs. Her hair almost fell to her shoulders in shimmering waves, and her make-up was expertly and freshly applied.

"Goin' out?"

"I was."

"Change of plans," I said, and stepped inside.

EIGHTEEN

"I didn't know anything about this."

We were seated on opposite ends of the sofa. She offered me a drink, but I turned it down. I wasn't there for a cocktail.

"Your husband hasn't said a word about it?"

"I don't think he knew, either."

"And neither Angela nor Sarah said a word to you?" I asked.

"I'm afraid my step-daughters never say a word to me, at all," she answered.

"Well, they spoke to me enough for both of us," I said.

"And you believe them?"

"If I believe you," I said, "that somebody is tryin' to kill your husband, why wouldn't I believe them that somebody's tryin' to kill them?"

"Because they're stupid, vapid girls."

"They're in their thirties," I said. "They're not girls."

"Well, they're certainly stupid," she said. "Look at the men they married."

"Tell me about that."

"About what?"

"This Piers guy. What's he like?"

"He's a thug," she said. "I think he's from Liverpool, or someplace as dreary. We warned her about marrying him."

"You both warned her?"

"Yes."

"So your husband and Piers don't like each other?"

"Not at all," Constance said. "Alan thought he was marrying Sarah for her money."

"Does she have money?"

"Some," she said. "Not as much as she will after Alan dies."

"Unless you get him to change his will."

"He'll never cut the girls out of his will," she said. "And I don't want him to. He'll be very generous with all of us."

"You just don't want him killed."

"Yes." She seemed sincere, but I had seen her apparently sincere before.

"And his daughters?"

"I don't want them dead, either."

"What about Angela's husband?"

"Harrison?" She seemed appalled. "He'd never have the balls!"

"But Piers would?"

"Oh yes," she said. "Believe me, I know his kind."

"Then I guess I'm gonna have to talk to Mr. Rohmer."

"What about my husband's business associates?" she asked.

"From what I understand," I said, "they would all like to see him dead. But right now it seems more likely the culprit is family."

"What happened to Angela and Sarah?"

I told her what they told me.

"Sarah's brakes?" she repeated. "That's too much of a coincidence, isn't it?"

"It seems like it."

"Where are they now?"

"Safe."

At that moment the phone rang. It was not her cell, but the hotel landline.

"Excuse me."

She got up, crossed the room and picked up the phone that was on the writing desk.

"Hello, Harrison. No, she's not here. No, I don't know where she is. Look, I can't talk, I'm with my detective...I hired him to keep Alan safe...John Headston. All right, when I see her, I'll tell her you're looking for her." She hung up and turned to me. "Harrison, looking for Angela."

"Did he say why?" I asked, as she came back over.

"No," she said, "only that he came home and she wasn't there."

"Did he sound worried?"

"Not especially," she said, coming back down on the sofa. "Maybe he's afraid she's out cheating on him."

"Is she the type?"

She made a rude noise with her mouth and said, "Definitely not. Now Sarah, maybe..."

"Really?" I asked. "She doesn't look the type. She looks... frail."

"I know," Constance said, "it makes men want to take care of her—which is what you're doing, right?"

"I'm doing what you hired me to do."

"I want you to keep my husband alive," she reminded me.

"And you're not worried about your step-daughters?"

She hesitated, then said, "Not as much as I am about my husband."

"Why did you tell Harrison you don't know where Angela is?" I asked.

"Because I don't."

"But you know I've got her someplace safe."

"I didn't think you'd want me to tell him," she said. "Should I have let you talk to him?"

"That might've been a good idea."

"Well," she said, "he was calling from home."

I hated retracing my steps, but going back to Angela's place to talk with her husband might have been the way to go, at the moment.

I stood up.

"Nothing else?" she asked, looking up at me as she remained

seated.

"Not right now," I said. "But what time will your husband be home?"

"He's got meetings all day," she said. "He won't be back until after eight. He told me not to wait for him to have dinner." She arched an eyebrow at me. "Interested? I can have something whipped up, and you could come back."

Truth be told, I wasn't even tempted. Carla might have been able to persuade me, but Constance had no such power over.

"No, thanks," I said, "but I may be back to talk to Alan."

"Should I tell him?"

"No, don't say a word," I said. "It'll be better if I catch him off guard."

She took a cigarette from a box on the table and lit it herself.

"You know the way out," she said.

NINETEEN

Constance hadn't put me under a full court press, but she had tested the waters. I was glad to find out she was completely out of my system.

When Harrison Wayne opened his door he said, "What?"

"Mr. Wayne, I'm John Headston."

"Where the hell is my wife?"

"In a safe place."

"Where?"

"Why don't we talk first?" I asked.

"Look," he said, pointing his finger at me, "if you don't tell me where—"

"Before I tell you anything, Mr. Wayne," I said, "I have to be sure you're not the one she's hiding from."

"What?" he said, taken aback. "You think—"

"Can I come in?"

He hesitated, then said, "Ah hell," turned and walked inside, leaving the door open. I followed, found him waiting in the large living room.

"What do you want, Headston?"

"How's your marriage, Mr. Wayne."

"It was fine," he said. "Look, you've got no right to keep me from my wife."

"Mr. Wayne," I said, "your wife has her cell phone. If she

wants to call you, she can."

"And you didn't tell her not to?"

"No, I didn't."

"This is crazy," he said. "Why would she think I want to harm her?"

"I don't know," I said. "That's what I'm tryin' to find out."

"But Angela didn't hire you."

"Constance hired me to keep Alan alive," I said. "She thinks somebody is gonna try and kill him."

"And what's that got to do with my wife?"

"I don't know," I said, "but if somebody's threatening both your wife and her sister, Sarah, it has to be connected to Alan, don't you think?"

Wayne thought a moment, then asked, "Do you want a drink?"

"Sure. I'll have whatever you're havin'."

He went to a small sidebar against the wall and poured two tumblers. When he handed it to me I smelled it first. It was bourbon. I took a sip. It was good bourbon.

He sat down across from me, his shoulders slumped.

"Why would Angela think I want to harm her?" he asked.

"She doesn't," I said, "but Sarah thinks her husband wants to kill her. I'm just tryin' to keep the father and daughters safe until I can figure out what the hell is goin' on."

"Now Piers," he said, "I can see him wanting to kill Sarah. Probably for insurance money."

"But not Angela or Alan?"

"Why?" Wayne asked. "That doesn't benefit him."

"What if he kills Alan and Angela," I said. "Then Sarah inherits everything, right?"

"There's still Constance," Wayne said. "And nobody's trying to kill her, are they?"

He had a good point there.

TWENTY

I finished my drink with Harrison Wayne and promised him I would have Angela call him.

"But I warn you, I'm gonna tell her not to say where she is. And that's as much for your benefit as hers."

"That's fine," he said, as he walked me to the door. "I just want to hear that she's safe."

I figured I could give him that.

My intention was to head back to Ally's place and talk to the two sisters again. However, something stopped me. It was a big man with large hands, who clamped them on my upper arms as soon as I exited the building.

"You are the private inquiry agent?" he asked, in a British accent, which immediately gave him away as Piers Rohmer, Sarah's husband.

"What if I am?" I asked.

"We need to talk."

I pulled myself from his grasp.

"I assume you're Piers Rohmer?"

"That's right."

"What do you and I need to talk about?"

"Not here," Rohmer said. "Not on the street."

"Do you have a weapon?" I asked.

"Why would I need a weapon?" he asked. "I just want to talk."

"Okay," I said, "there's a diner around the corner. Let's go there."

"Fine."

It was actually a little more than around the corner, on Amsterdam Avenue, that we stopped in a diner and got a booth. We each ordered a cup of coffee and, at the last minute, I added a donut.

"What's on your mind, Mr. Rohmer?" I asked.

"Well, for one thing," he said, "I'm thinking you know where my wife is."

"Is your wife missing?"

"Not missing," he said, "but she's gone. I know she took a plane here, and I was thinking she went to see her sister."

"Is that why you were outside the building?" I asked.

"I thought I might see her coming out."

"But you saw me," I said. "How do you know who I am, and why would you think I know where your wife is?"

"She mentioned your name," he said. "I did some research, saw your photo online. I know your history."

"I see."

"None of which matters right now," he added, which pleased me. I wasn't about to discuss my background with him.

"So when I saw you come out of the building, I just decided we needed to talk."

"And here we are." I took a bite of my donut, washed it down with some coffee.

"What did my wife tell you?"

"I haven't seen your wife, Mr. Rohmer," I lied. "My client is Constance Pennyworth."

"My bitch stepmother-in-law," he said.

"Whatever she is to you," I said, "she's my client. She thinks somebody might be tryin' to harm her husband."

"Like who?"

"I don't know," I said. "Why don't you tell me?"

"How would I know who—wait a minute," he said, looking shocked as something just occurred to him. "You think it's me?"

"Again," I said, "I don't know. Do you have anythin' against Alan Pennyworth?"

"Just whatever a son-in-law has against a father-in-law who doesn't respect him," he said. "But that's not enough to harm him, or kill him. If that was the case, there would be no fathers-in-law left."

"That's probably true."

"I think you better look at Alan's business contacts," Rohmer went on. "That's where you're going to find somebody who wants to hurt him."

"Good advice," I said. "Now, why don't you tell me how things are between you and your wife? Why would she take a plane to New York without tellin' you why?"

"I don't have the slightest idea," Rohmer said. "I do know that her family—especially her sister—has never liked me, and perhaps she finally listened to what that bitch Angela had to say."

"So her step-mother and sister are both bitches?"

"Exactly."

"And her father?"

"A sonofabitch."

"Jesus," I said, "what about your brother-in-law?"

"He's a little stuck-up, but not a bad guy."

"Well, at least you have somethin' nice to say about somebody," I said. "I don't wanna hear what your opinion of me is."

"That'll depend on whether or not you tell me where my wife is," Rohmer said, truthfully.

"She can tell you where she is," I said, "if she wants to."

He stared at me, and I had the feeling he could get mean if he wanted to. I thought I remembered Angela telling me he'd been a hood in England—no, a thug from Liverpool, that was it. Although if he had a Liverpool—Liverpuddlin'?—accent, he was hiding it.

I watched him, and I thought he wrangled it in.

"Look, here's my card," I said, handing it to him. "Are you gonna stay in the city?"

"Until I find my wife, yes."

"Stay in touch with me," I said. "If I can help you, I will. Fair enough?"

"I suppose it will have to be," he said.

TWENTY-ONE

I felt I needed to talk to the head of the family again. This time much more in depth. I called Constance on her cell and told her I wanted to talk to Alan, again.

"He's been trying to get me to fire you," she said. "He won't let me pay you unless you come up with something."

"Well, I have," I said, "and I want to talk to you both about it."

"Now?"

"Right now."

"Well, we're getting dressed for dinner," she said. "How soon can you get here?"

"Fifteen minutes."

"I'll try to stall him until you arrive."

"Aren't you gonna tell him I'm coming?"

"No," she said, and hung up.

I usually got around Manhattan on foot or by subway. For this I hailed a cab.

I knocked on the door of their Four Seasons room seventeen minutes later.

"You're late," Constance said.

"You don't look ready," I commented.

"I still have to do my hair."

"That's good," I said, entering the suite. "I want to talk to your husband."

"He's in here."

She took me to a sitting room where Alan Pennyworth was lounging on a sofa. He was dressed for dinner.

"I'll be ten minutes," she said, and went into what I assumed was a bedroom.

"I might need more time than that," I told Pennyworth.

"Don't worry," he said, "she'll be at least another half hour, maybe more."

"You'll miss your reservation."

He smiled.

"Our reservations are an hour later than I tell Constance," he said. "That's the only way I can be sure we'll ever make them. Have a seat, Mr. Headston. Can I get you something from the bar?"

"No, thank you," I said, sitting in a soft armchair across from him. "I just need to talk to you."

"About Constance?"

"About your whole family."

"My daughters?"

"And your sons-in-law."

"Oh, them."

"How much do you dislike them?" I asked. "Because I need some honest answers from you, right now."

"Intensely," he said, "but I'm nothing if not honest, so go ahead. Ask your questions."

"Constance seems to think someone is trying to kill you."

"I'm aware of that fact."

"Your daughter feels someone is trying to kill her, and she thinks it might be her husband."

"Angela and Harrison?"

"No, Sarah and Piers."

Alan frowned.

"There's not much difference—except that I don't think Harrison's the type. Cheat, yes. Kill? No."

"But Piers?"

"He spent years as a thug in London," Alan said. "Now he's taught himself what fork to use and married my daughter. But he's still a thug."

"Why would he want to kill Sarah?"

"For her money, naturally."

"Okay, so if he's trying to kill her, is he also trying to kill you?"

"Why would he do that?"

"Well, since we're talking about money, if you died how much would Sarah get?"

"If that's his game," Alan said, "he'd kill me first so that she inherited, and then kill her."

"Right," I said, "but according to Sarah, someone's already tried to kill her."

"How?" he asked. "How did they try?"

"Twice with a car," I said. "Once her brakes were tampered with, and once a car tried to run her down."

"And my brakes were tampered with," Alan said. "Could it be the same guy? Piers?"

"Maybe."

"But why kill her before he kills me?" Alan asked.

"Sarah did say she thought Piers would have her killed and just take what he could get."

"Okay, so that means he's not the one trying to kill me."

"No, I don't like that one, either," I said.

"Why not?"

"It's too much of a coincidence."

"And what about Angela?" Alan asked. "Is somebody trying to kill her?"

"No," I said, "well, not yet, but right now I've got her and Sarah hidden away."

"That's good. And how's Harrison acting?"

"He's looking for her. Says he's worried."

"Maybe he is," Alan sad. "I mean, it would definitely be too much of a coincidence if each of my daughter's husbands were trying to have them killed."

"Yes, it would be," I said, "unless…"

"Unless what?"

"What if they're working together?" I asked. "What if Harrison just hasn't gotten around to making an actual attempt on Angela?"

"So you're saying Harrison and Piers could be working together to try and kill me and my daughters."

"I guess I'm here to ask what you think of that possibility."

Alan drummed his fingers on the arm of the sofa for a few seconds, giving the question some thought.

"In my business I read people," he said. "I can believe Piers would hill Sarah, but I don't believe Harrison would kill Angela."

"Are they in love?"

"Which ones?"

"Any of them."

"Angela loves Harrison," he said, "of that I'm sure. And Sarah loved Piers when she married him three years ago."

"Not anymore?"

"Piers is a dick," Alan said.

Constance came into the room at that point.

"Have you resolved anything?" she asked.

"I think we've been going in circles," I said. "Probably my fault." I stood up.

"Are you any closer to finding out who's trying to kill Alan?"

"No," I said, "and now it seems someone's trying to kill Sarah."

"Sarah?" Constance asked. "She's so sweet. I can understand someone wanting to kill Angela, but not Sarah."

"Constance," Alan said, wearily.

"What? I'm sorry, darling, but Angela is kind of a bitch."

"Can you see Harrison wanting to kill her?" I asked her.

"Harrison?" She looked taken aback. "He cheats on her, but

I don't see him wanting to kill her. Oh, I see, with Sarah it's Piers...well, yeah, him I can see stooping that low." She looked around. "Where are they?"

"Hidden away," Alan said "Mr. Headston is looking after them."

She walked to him and put her hand on his shoulder.

"And who's looking after you, darling?"

"I believe you and I are leaving that in Mr. Headston's hands as well, my dear." He stood up. "Only I'm not going to be hidden away. Let me get my jacket and we'll go to dinner."

"Maybe Mr. Headston should come along," she called after him, as he left the room. She turned and looked at me. "Johnny?"

"I can't look for the killer and bodyguard your husband, Constance," I said. "Which do you want?"

"I want you to find who's doing this and put a stop to it."

"Okay then..." I headed for the door. "You enjoy your dinner."

"Johnny," she said, again.

"What?"

She put her hand to her throat, just laid it there.

"You don't think I'm in any danger, do you?"

"No," I said, and as I left I thought, not yet.

TWENTY-TWO

I had to admit the men in the Pennyworth family did not seem like a particularly loving bunch. But the more I thought about it, neither did the women. Constance called her husband by certain endearments, but I had the distinct feeling she felt closer to his money than to him.

I decided to go to Ally's loft to speak to the two Pennyworth sisters again. Maybe they had put their heads together and thought of something that could set me on the right track.

When Ally opened her door to let me in the scent of orange chicken and fried rice hit me in the face.

"We saved you some," she said, seeing the hungry look that must've been on my face.

"Thanks," I said, entering. "I'm starving."

Sarah Rohmer and Angela Wayne both looked up at me as Ally and I reached the sofa/loveseat area of her loft. Against the far back wall was a bedroom set-up. There was a bevy of Chinese food cartons spread out on the coffee table before them. Also on the table were bottles of various different brands of iced tea.

"Ladies."

"Come and join us," Angela said. "We have enough for a feast."

Sarah only nodded as she chewed on what looked like lo mein.

The two sisters were sitting on the soda. Ally lowered herself onto one side of the loveseat. Since the other side was facing away from the table of food, I sat in a nearby armchair. All three pieces of furniture matched, and cost more than my entire apartment.

"Just pick a carton," Ally said.

I leaned forward, peered into them and found the one I had smelled at the door, the orange chicken. Although the girls were eating out of the cartons, there were plates on the table. Also, they were using chop sticks, but there were forks. I picked one up, scooped out some orange chicken, then added some fried rice to my plate and sat back.

"Snapple, Lipton or Pure Leaf?" Ally asked.

"I don't know...water?"

"Bottled or tap?"

"Tap," I said, "with ice."

She leaped up off her loveseat and said, "Comin' up, boss."

"Does she have to call you that?" Angela asked.

"No," I said, "but she thinks it's funny."

"She's a smart young lady," Sarah said.

"Yes, she is."

Ally came back and handed me a tall glass of water with ice, then sat back down.

"Thank you," I said, setting it down on the table. Then I sat back and started to eat.

"So what did you do today?" Angela asked.

"I spoke to your husbands, and your father."

"And?" Sarah asked.

"I don't know which of them I found colder," I said.

Angela laughed.

"That's about the only thing those three have in common."

"Well," I said, "your husbands did seem to want to know where you were."

"Did they ask how we are?" Angela asked.

"Harrison did," I told her. "In fact, he wants you to call him and let him know you're all right."

"And Piers?" Sarah asked.

"He wants to know where you are."

"Yeah, so he can kill me."

"Sarah—" Angela said.

"Who else would want me dead?" her sister asked.

"It doesn't make any sense," Angela said. "It's not like he'd get a lot of money if you were dead."

"But if your father died first," I said, "and left you girls his money—"

"But he'd never leave it to us," Sarah said. "He'd leave it to Constance."

"All of it?" I asked.

"Probably not," Angela said. "We'd each get some."

"Enough for Rohmer to kill your sister?"

"Maybe," Angela said.

"Oh, God," Sarah whined.

"But right now there's no money," Angela said, putting a hand on her sister's knee. "There's no reason for him to kill you."

"So, what then?" Sarah asked. "Accidents?"

"No accidents where your father is concerned," I said. "Somebody's trying to kill him."

Angela put her carton down.

"Okay," she said, "what about Piers trying to kill father?"

"Why?" I asked.

"Because he doesn't know how much money will come to Sarah," Angela said. "But he's making an investment."

I chewed on a piece of chicken and swallowed.

"That could be," I said, "but it doesn't explain the attempts on Angela."

"Well then," she said, picking up her carton again, "Constance is paying you to find the answers—find them!"

"And what will you do in the meantime?" I asked.

"I'll go back home," she said, "and I'll take my sister with me. We'll be safe there. You said so yourself, Harrison's worried about me."

"Yes."

"I'll call him," she said. "I'll be able to tell from his voice if we should go."

"And what about Piers?" Sarah asked. "I still don't think I want to see him."

"Then you won't," Angela said. "Not until you want to."

I started looking around the table.

"Whataya need, boss?" Ally asked.

"Is there any soy sauce?"

TWENTY-THREE

"Did they go?" I asked Ally, as she came into the office the next morning.

"They did," she said. "Angela called her husband and was convinced they'd be safe."

"Then I'm back to square one," I said. "Who's trying to kill Alan Pennyworth?"

"And why?"

"Who is more important than why," I told her.

"But if you knew why, wouldn't that help you with the who?" she asked.

"Probably."

"So let me help," she said. "What do we do first?"

"I don't know," I said. "I'll have to think about it. I've already talked to everyone in the family."

"Well," she said, "I've got some filing to do. Lemme know if you need me."

"I will."

I left her at her desk and went into my office to sit at mine. The only person to talk to about Alan Pennyworth's business practices was Constance. Not that I really wanted to talk with her again, but what choice did I have? I had the chance to turn the case down and didn't take it. Now I was involved.

I picked up the phone and called Constance.

"Do you have something?" she asked.

"No more than I had the last time we talked."

"Then why did you wake me up?"

I looked at my watch. It was nine-fifteen a.m. Time for me to open my office, but wealthy people like Constance didn't have any reason to be up that early, if they didn't want to be.

"I'm on my way over," I said. "Order some coffee. I'll see you in fifteen."

"Johnny…"

"What?"

She sighed.

"Make it half an hour."

"Right."

When Constance finally opened the door after I'd pounded on it for a while, she was wearing a silk robe over her lace nightgown, still looking like she'd just gotten out of bed. Except that she had run a brush or something through her hair.

"You went back to bed," I said.

"Don't worry," she said. "I called for room service first." She turned and allowed me to enter. "I remembered you liked Spanish omelets." She turned her back and looked out a window.

I'd had coffee and a bagel on the way to my office, but an omelet sounded good.

"Sorry I haven't had time to put my face on."

"You look fine."

She turned and faced me again.

"Do I? That's sweet."

"Where's Mr. Pennyworth?"

"He left earlier for a business meeting."

"He keeps working," I said. "Isn't he afraid there'll be another attempt?"

"He says he can't hide," she said. "Besides, he trusts you to find out who's doing it and stop them."

"Does he?"

"He likes you."

"I couldn't tell."

"He doesn't show things like that," she said. "But I can see it."

There was a knock at the door.

"That'll be room service," she said, starting for it.

"I'll get it," I said, putting my hand out to stop her.

When I opened the door there was a dapper man in a hotel uniform standing behind a breakfast cart.

"Your breakfast, sir," he said.

"Bring it right in."

I backed away to let him wheel it in.

"Shall I set the table, sir?"

"No," I said, "I've got it."

"Then just sign, please." He held out a black leather folder with the bill. I took it and gave it to Constance, who signed it.

"Thank you, sir," he said, as I returned it. "Enjoy your morning."

He left and pulled the door closed behind him.

I brought two chairs over to the cart and we sat across from each other and removed the cloches. She had ordered full breakfasts for both of us: omelets, potatoes, toast, coffee and juice.

"I remembered how we used to enjoy room service together," she said.

"That was years ago, Constance," I said. "We were different people."

"I was," she said, "but you're the same, Johnny."

"Hardly."

I cut into my omelet with my fork.

"Let's not talk about the past," I said.

"Then what shall we talk about?" she asked. "Why are you here?"

"Still trying to figure out who's trying to kill your husband."

"And what about the girls?"

"They're safe," I said.

"So you don't believe Sarah when she says someone is trying to kill her?" she asked.

"It doesn't make sense," I said, "but yes, I believe her."

"Why doesn't it make sense?"

"Because it makes sense to kill her father first, and then her," I said.

"You think it's her husband?"

"She thinks it's her husband. Right now, I've got no reason to suspect him. Unless you tell me how much your husband is leaving to each of his daughters when he passes."

"Nothing."

"Nothing?"

"Not if I have anything to say about it," she said.

I suddenly lost my appetite.

"Have you talked with Piers?"

"Have you talked to him?"

"I have," I said. "He's here in New York, and says he just wants to know where she is."

"Then is he going to try to kill Alan?"

"I doubt it."

I had eaten half the omelet while we talked. Now I put my fork down, wiped my mouth with the white cloth napkin, and stood up.

"I came here to get some names from you, Constance," I said. "Anybody you think might want to kill your husband."

"What about the girls?" she asked.

"His own daughters?" I said. "First you'd cheat them out of any inheritance, and then put them up as possible suspects trying to murder their father?"

"Do you think they're little angels?" she asked.

"Constance," I said, "I don't think I can work for you anymore."

"Johnny."

"I thought this morning that I had my chance to turn you

95

down, but didn't take it," I said. "But this is my chance to walk away, and I'm outta here."

"Johnny—"

"You were right," I said. "I haven't changed that much. I almost let you make a fool of me...again."

I left before she had a chance to say my name again.

"You did what?" Ally asked.

I was back in my office, with my feet up on my desk.

"I quit," I said.

"Why?"

"Because I saw her for what she is," I explained.

"Why do I have the feeling there's more to it than that?" she asked. "More to the story of you and Constance Pennyworth."

"Carla," I said.

"What?"

"Her real name is Carla," I said, "and it was a long time ago..."

PART THREE

TWENTY-FOUR

Six Months Later...

Dominick "Sugar" Garbanzo hadn't changed much.

When we were kids we called him "Sugar Garbanzo Beans." We stopped when he grew big enough to kick our asses.

Sugar made his way up the ladder in the New York families while I was doing everything to screw up my life and career. Now I had gotten word he wanted to see me, and when you got the word from Sugar, you usually responded. But there were still some people in town who didn't know who he was.

"What," Ally asked, coming into my office, "is a Sugar Garbanzo?"

"A friend of mine from when we were kids," I said. "He grew up to be a killer."

"Really?" She gaped at me.

"Well," I said, "he's gotten to the point in his career where other people do his killing for him."

"But...he killed people?"

"A few, in his younger days as a button man for the Mafia."

"But...I thought there was no more Mafia."

"They're still around, though not to the degree they used to be. And that really doesn't matter to Dom. He's on his own, now. Why do you ask?"

"You got a message from him," she said. "A gravelly voice

on the phone said you should meet him for lunch today at noon."

She approached my desk and handed me a message slip with the name of the restaurant on it.

"Okay, thanks."

"Are you going?" she asked.

"Well, an invitation from Sugar isn't really an invitation," I said. "It's a summons. So yeah, I'm going."

"So...you're friends with a big New York gangster?"

"I haven't seen Dom in a while," I said. "I guess I'll find out today whether or not we're still friends."

The Mafia's influence and connection to Little Italy had faded away in recent years, and it's now a neighborhood that features bus and walking tours. Chinatown is a more palpable presence all around Little Italy, and they actually intertwine in some spots, but Sugar Garbanzo still called it home.

There was no mob connection whatsoever with Rocky's, the Italian restaurant on the corner of Mulberry and Spring Streets. To show you how eclectic things had become, down the street was Eight Mile Creek, an Australian restaurant that served, among other things, kangaroo. But Rocky's was where I was supposed to meet with Sugar.

I entered and spotted him sitting alone at a back table. There were no torpedoes with him, which would have been the case in old Little Italy.

He saw me and stood up, and the only thing that kept him from looking like the Hulk was the fact he wasn't green. Sugar had a huge growth spurt between grammar school and high school, and as a freshman he scared the bejesus out of everyone from freshmen to seniors.

"Hey, Johnny," he said, as I approached his table. I stuck my hand out, but he surprised me by grabbing me in a bear hug that almost lifted me off my feet.

"Siddown, brother," he said, taking his own seat. Once he

was seated people stopped staring. That happens to a huge block of a man in a track suit when he stands up in the middle of a restaurant. Especially if the track suit is yellow, with blue stripes down the sleeves and pants.

"How you been, Dom?" I asked. "It's been a lot of years."

"I know it," he said. "I heard about some of the bullshit you had to go through. I've had my fair share of shit, too, but now I'm a legitimate businessman."

"That's what I heard," I said. We both ignored the fact that 'the bullshit' I went through was thanks to his referral.

"You know," he said, "in the old days I wouldn't have been able to sit here without thinking somebody was waiting to fill me fulla lead. But now I can just sit here and eat."

As if on cue a waiter came to the table and set an antipasto platter down in the center.

"I hope you don't mind," Sugar said, "I ordered the appetizer."

"That's fine with me."

We both put some on our small plates and started to eat.

"You ever eat down the street?" I asked him.

"The Australian place? Sure."

"Kangaroo?"

"Tastes like a cross between venison and buffalo meat," he said.

"I'll pass."

"How've you been, Johnny?"

"Okay."

"You gettin' your business back up and runnin'?"

"The office is open."

"How many operatives you got workin' for you, these days?"

"One," I said. "Me." Before he could go any further I asked, "What's with the lunch, Dom?"

"You're still the only one who calls me 'Dom,'" he pointed out.

"Do you prefer 'Garbanzo?'" I asked. "Or one of the other colorful names they used to call you back in grammar school?"

"Nope," he said, "Dom's fine."

"Then what's on your mind?"

"Let's order lunch," he said, as the waiter returned, "and I'll tell you."

"Order for the both of us," I said.

"You like seafood?"

"No."

He ordered spaghetti with garlic and oil for me, calamari for himself and a Peroni beer for both of us.

"Okay," he said, reaching for the antipasto plate again, "let's get down to it."

"Down to what?"

"I need a favor, Johnny."

I hadn't expected that. A job, maybe, but not a favor.

"Not that you owe me anythin'," Sugar said, "'cause you don't. The favor I want is for you to take a job from me."

"I thought you went legit?" I asked.

"I am legit," he said. "I need your talents as an investigator."

"There are a lot of top agencies in Manhattan, Sugar," I said. "Why me?"

"Because we go back a long way. I trust you. You ain't never fucked me, and I don't think I ever fucked you." He thought a moment. "Have I?"

"Well," I said, "there was that time, sophomore year—"

"Ah, Mary-Ann Jonkowski," he said, with a fond look. "Come on, man...you woulda fucked me if you could. Or her!"

"Yeah, I would've," I said. "Okay, let's hear it."

"Not many people know this," he said, "but I have a daughter."

"What?" I was shocked. Sugar Garbanzo was not the fatherly type. "When did you get married?"

"Never," Sugar said. "Lacy's my love child."

"Dom—"

"I know, I know." he said, waving away my comments, "it's a stupid term, but it sounds better than 'illegitimate.'"

I couldn't argue with that.

"How old is she?" I asked.

"Seventeen."

"Wow," I said, "and all this time I never heard a whisper."

"I know," he said, "I've kept it quiet. You want that last piece of pepperoni?"

"No, go ahead."

He snagged it from the plate in the middle of the table. The bus boy must have been hovering, because he darted forward and grabbed the empty.

"Excuse me," Sugar said, "I'm nervous talkin' about this."

I was shocked again. Ever since our freshman year at Canarsie High School in Brooklyn, I had never seen Sugar nervous.

"Relax, Dom," I said. "Just talk to me."

"Johnny," he said, "Lacy's missin'. I want you to find 'er."

TWENTY-FIVE

"Missin'?" I asked. "Or kidnapped?"

"I don't know which I'd like it to be," Sugar admitted. "If she's been kidnapped, it's by somebody I used to do business with."

"From the other side of the law."

"Right."

"And if she's missin'?"

Sugar looked pained.

"Then it means she left on her own."

"Or?"

"Or what?"

"Come on, Dom, there's an 'or' in there, somewhere."

The pained look increased.

"Or she left with a boy."

"Ah."

"But not a boy," he went on, "an asshole who's too old for her."

"Have you asked him?"

"I don't know where he is, either."

"Ah…"

The waiter came with our orders and we suspended the conversation until he left. I also noticed that there was no one seated at the tables surrounding us. We were effectively ensconced in a cone of silence from other diners. I was sure Sugar had something to do with this.

We continued to talk while we ate and drank. I covered my spaghetti with a layer of parmesan cheese and dug in.

"Do you know this guy's name?"

"Yeah," Sugar said, "he goes by Tommy O, but his name's Oronotti."

"Italian," I said. "What a surprise. Do you know his family?"

"No," Sugar said, "I don't know where he comes from. He just...appeared."

"Appeared?" I asked. "Or was he planted?"

"That thought had occurred to me," he admitted. "But why would somebody from my old life come after me now? And why go after my daughter? And how'd they find out about her?"

"From her mother?"

"Her mother and me, we get along," Sugar said. "I send her money every month. She wouldn't risk that."

"Not even for more money?"

He chewed what was in his mouth, swallowed and said, "That's what you're gonna find out for me."

That almost sounded like an order.

"You mean," I said, "if I decide to do you this favor."

"Right, right," he said, "that's what I meant."

I relayered my pasta with parmesan.

"Where is she missin' from?" I asked.

"A private school uptown," he said.

"High school or college?"

"High school."

"What happened?"

"A couple of mornings ago they went to wake her, and she wasn't in her bed."

"Does she have a roommate?" I asked.

"Yes, but the girl claims they went to sleep at the same time the night before, and she didn't wake up until they came to the door to fetch them."

"So it looked as if they both overslept?"

"Right."

"Was the roommate checked for a drug?"

"I thought of that. She wasn't, and it's too late now. Any drug would be out of her system."

"Do you have any idea where Lacy might have gone, if she went on her own?"

"No," he said.

"And if she was kidnapped?"

"It could be anybody I used to do business with."

"Or just opportunistic kidnappers," I offered. "You've had no ransom demands?"

"None."

I never understood how people could eat squid, but he was consuming his calamari with vigor.

"So there's three possibilities," I said. "She left on her own, she was kidnapped by an old enemy, or kidnapped by strangers."

"Right."

"So why did you only mention two possibilities, Dom?" I asked. "You're not crediting strangers, at all."

He stopped eating and stared at me.

"Tell me why she might leave on her own?" I asked.

"She didn't like the school she was in."

"She's seventeen," I said. "How many more semesters did she have?"

"She's a junior," Sugar said.

"What about college?"

"Oh, she's goin'," he said, firmly.

"Dom, does this girl even know you're her father?"

"I told you, it's a secret...even from her."

"And what if she finds out that Dominick Garbanzo is her father?" I asked. "What if she already knows, and she's actin' out?"

"Who'd tell 'er? Her mother would never do that."

"What about Tommy?"

"How would he know?"

"Good question."

Sugar ate the last of his calamari and pushed the plate away. The busboy ran over to get the empty plate.

"Leave it!" Sugar snapped.

"Sorry, sir," the boy said, "I thought you were done."

"I am," Sugar said, "but my friend's not. Just wait til we're both finished."

"Yessir!" the boy said, and scurried away.

"I hate that!" Sugar said.

"Dom," I said, "I'll do what I can."

"Oh, Johnny, that's great," he said. "And I'm gonna pay ya. Any amount."

"The going rate is fine," I said. "I'll bill you. But Dom, I'll have to talk to the mother."

"Yeah," he said, "yeah, I figured that. But...she's got her own family, now. I think that's why she sent Lacy away to school. Maybe you don't have to talk to her."

"We'll see, Dom."

"Just make sure when you find Lacy, she doesn't know I'm her father, okay?"

"I'll do my best."

I finished and pushed my plate away. Sugar waved over the busboy, who cleared both plates with a worried look.

"Tiramisu?" Sugar asked.

"Sure, why not?" I said. "But Dom...who's the mother?"

"Who else?" he asked. "Mary-Ann Jonkowski."

TWENTY-SIX

This was my year for women coming out of my past. First Carla Balducci as Constance Pennyworth, and now Mary-Ann Jonkowski.

"You dog," I said. "How did that happen?"

"We ran into each other about eighteen years ago—hey, it was a high school reunion and you didn't come."

"I was busy elsewhere," I said.

"Well, it was an old cliché one-night stand. We both had too much to drink, didn't see each other for a few months until she called and told me she was pregnant—and she was having it. Didn't expect anything from me except maybe some money."

"And you gave it to her."

"Every month since then."

"Every month?" I asked, surprised.

"Hey, Lacy's my kid, Johnny."

I didn't want to tell him I thought he could've got away with a one-time lump sum payment, but I did think it. My memory of Mary-Ann Jonkowski was sweet smelling, lots of hair, big boobs, creamy skin, and a reputation for being loose. I was too shy at the time to find out just how loose. I did tell Sugar once that I was going to ask her out to a high school dance, but he got there first. Hence the one time he had fucked me.

"Wait a minute," I said. "The night you took her to that

Brooklyn Tech dance, you told me you scored."

He looked sheepish.

"Okay, that time I lied," he said, "but fourteen years later I did. She still had all that blond hair, and those huge knockers."

Sugar still had a head like a block of cement—but with much less hair—and underneath his running suit he looked to have gone to fat somewhat, but maybe eighteen years ago, under the influence, he'd looked good.

"Okay," I said, "I need the name and address of the school, who to talk to there and Mary-Ann's address."

He reached down under his chair, came up with a manila folder and held it out to me.

"It's all in there."

The folder felt pretty thick.

"What else is in here?"

"Just some thoughts," he said. "Some names of people I think might be behind it, if it's a snatch."

"Am I gonna be up against some old-time mob guys on this, Dom?"

"Naw, naw," he said, "just some old business associates."

"So no badda-bing, badda-boom guys?"

He shrugged.

"Maybe one or two."

"Jesus."

The waiter brought two tiramisus and two coffees just in time. I needed the comfort of those whipped cream and coffee-soaked ladyfingers.

When I left the restaurant Sugar said he was going to stay and have another cup of coffee. But I knew he didn't want to go out on the street alone, so he'd wait for some of his men to come and get him. He was about as legit as a three-dollar bill.

Once outside I walked three blocks to the Canal Street subway station and took the train back uptown. I got a seat because it was midday and nobody was going home or to work. I opened the folder Sugar had given me and familiarized myself with the locations of the school Lacy had disappeared from, and Mary-Ann's address. The school was uptown, on Ninety-Second Street, while Mary-Ann still lived in Brooklyn.

Sugar's other list, the one comprised of the names of his old mob friends and enemies who might've kidnapped his daughter, was long and tedious reading. I was going to save judgment on whether or not she was kidnapped until after I talked to the people at the school.

My first intention had been to return to my office after lunch, but instead I remained on the train until Ninety-Second Street, then walked the few blocks to St. Mary's School for Girls. No wonder Lacy had disappeared. A Catholic girl's school like this was such a throwback.

I went through the front door and encountered a hallway full of teenagers, in uniform. I hadn't seen girls in such outfits since I attended a dance at Bishop Kearny High School my senior year, thirty-two years ago. It made me feel like I'd gone back in time.

"Excuse me," I said to two thirteen or fourteen-year-olds who were passing by.

"Yes sir?"

"Can either of you tell me where the principal's office is?"

"We don't have a principal, sir," one girl said. "But Mrs. Fenster is our headmistress."

That was the name I had in the folder Sugar had given me, but he hadn't provided her title.

"And where can I find her?" I asked.

The first girl started to answer, but the second girl—a smart looking blonde—put her hand on the mousy brunette's arm.

"Why?" she asked.

"I'm a private investigator," I said. "I'm here to talk to her about a case."

Both their eyes went wide.

"You're a private eye?" the brunette asked.

"I am."

The blonde seemed to be trying to rein herself in.

"You don't look like a private eye," she said.

"What do I look like?"

They glanced at each other, and the brunette seemed embarrassed.

"A teacher," the blonde said.

"Oh, that can't be good."

"If you go down this hall to the end, sir," the brunette said, "and then turn right you'll find the headmistress's office."

"Thank you."

The girls in the hallway all gave me long, curious looks as I passed or walked along with them. As a teenager those plaid uniformed skirts on the Catholic girls did nothing for me, and things hadn't changed.

TWENTY-SEVEN

I found the headmistress's office, stepped aside to let two girls leave, and then entered. A small, middle-aged woman looked up sternly at me from behind her desk. The name plate on her desk said MISS BODEEN. No title. Behind her was a closed door with HEADMISTRESS on it.

"Can I help you?"

"Yes, I'd like to see Mrs. Fenster."

"The headmistress is very busy," she said. "Do you have an appointment, Mister—"

"Headston," I said. "I'm a private investigator and, no, I don't have an appointment."

"Then I'm afraid it's impossible for you to see—"

"It's about Lacy..." I trailed off because I wasn't sure what Lacy's last name was, so I went for it. "...Jonkowski."

That did it.

"Oh, you're a detective, you said?"

"Private detective."

"I see. Are you working for the family?"

"I am."

"Please wait a moment."

She stood up and I saw she was wearing a severely cut gray suit. She turned and went into her boss's office. After a few moments she came out, but kept the door open.

"Mrs. Fenster will see you, Mr. Headstone."

I didn't correct her.

"Thank you."

I walked past her into the office. She closed the door behind me.

A tall, slender, attractive woman in her forties stood up behind her desk and smiled at me. She wore large, black-framed glasses, her dark hair in a bun.

"Mr. Headstone?" she asked.

"Headston."

"I'm sorry," she said. "Headston. I'm Helen Fenster, the headmistress of Saint Mary's."

She extended her hand. I approached her desk and shook it.

"Please, have a seat," she said, reseating herself.

I sat across from her in a stiff visitor's chair. It was probably deliberate. She didn't want students to be comfortable when they came to see her.

"You're here about Lacy?"

"That's right," I said. "Her...family wants me to determine if she left on her own, or was taken."

"Taken?" she asked, frowning. "You mean...kidnapped?"

"Yes."

"But...how could that be?"

"Do you have security here?"

"Well...no. We've never seen the need for...do you mean armed security?"

"Yes," I said. "With school shootings the way they are—"

"This is a girl's catholic institution," she said, cutting me off. "Have you ever heard of a case of a shooting incident, by a girl?"

"Well," I said, "without any security, a kidnapping might have taken place."

"How can you find out?" she asked.

"First," I said, "I need to talk with you, and then with Lacy's roommate."

"What do you want from me?"

"What was Lacy's state of mind before she disappeared?"

"That's hard to say," she said. "I don't see the students on a day-to-day basis."

"Was she a good student?"

"Excellent."

"Had her grades dipped recently?"

"I don't believe so, but we can check." She touched her intercom. "Miriam, please get me Lacy Jonkowski's records."

"Yes, ma'am."

"If she was kidnapped, why aren't the police here?" she asked. "Or the FBI?"

"Once it's determined that it was a kidnapping, they will be," I said. "Haven't the police been here at all?"

"No."

That probably made some kind of warped sense. Sugar wouldn't contact the police, and he probably didn't let Mary-Ann. So except for me, right now nobody was looking for this kid.

According to Sugar's folder, she had disappeared two days ago. My guess was he had spent those two days trying to find her, then decided to call me in.

"Did she have any trouble with any of the other students?"

"Trouble?"

"Did she have any enemies?"

"Enemies?" she seemed shocked by the question. "She's a seventeen-year-old girl."

"Was she ever in here for fighting, or anything like that?"

"No."

"Detention?"

"We don't give girls detention," she said. "We don't feel it's educational."

"Really?"

Miss Bodeen came in, handed her a folder, and left. Mrs. Fenster opened it, studied it a moment, then said, "No drop in her grades." She closed it and left it on the top of her desk with her hands folded it.

"Can I see that folder?" I asked.

"I'm afraid not," she said. "We are, after all, a private school—the emphasis being on 'private.'"

"I understood she wasn't happy about bein' here."

"Who told you that?" she asked. "All our girls love it here."

"It's a school, isn't it?"

"Of course."

"It's my experience that kids don't love school."

"Is there anything else I can tell you, Mr. Headston?"

"Yes," I said, "her family thinks she might have run off with a boy named Tommy. Do you know him?"

"No."

"Have any boys ever been caught in the dorm rooms?"

"We don't allow it."

"I know," I said, "but have you ever caught any?"

"What's that got to do with this?"

"I see," I said. "So you have caught boys up there."

"I told you," she said, "we don't have security."

"But somebody's in charge, right?"

"The dorm supervisor."

"A teacher?"

"Sometimes it's a teacher, sometimes it's one of the older girls."

"And who is it this day?"

"One of the seniors."

"Then I'll need to talk to her right after I talk to Lacy's roommate."

"And me?"

"I'll probably need to talk to you, again, at some point," I said. "But I'm ready for her roommate, now."

"I'll have Miss Bodeen locate her and bring her here," she said, getting up. "Excuse me."

She left the room. Immediately, I grabbed Lacy's file from her desk. It made for interesting reading.

TWENTY-EIGHT

Lacy's roommate was a girl named Angelica Rogers. She was a pretty redhead whose freckles were going to take her far.

When Mrs. Fenster brought the girl into her office I had the folder back where she'd left it.

"Angelica, this is Mr. Headston," she said. "He wants to ask you some questions about Lacy."

"Sure," Angelica said, with a shrug.

"Thank you, Mrs. Fenster," I said, "for the use of your office." She stared at me a moment, then got it.

"I'll give you some privacy," she said. "But I'll be right outside."

As soon as she was gone the girl's demeanor changed. She had entered the room in a slouch, but now she straightened up. The white blouse and plaid skirt did nothing to hide her figure when she did that. It was amazing. She walked across the room sat on a leather sofa Fenster kept by the window, and crossed her legs so I could see her thighs and calves clearly.

"Thanks for makin' her leave," she said. "Now we can relax."

"Do all the girls slouch around the Headmistress?" I asked. She smiled.

"Only the ones who're built."

"Like you?"

"You noticed."

"How old are you, Angelica?"

"Seventeen goin' on thirty," she said, proudly.

"Was Lacy also seventeen goin' on thirty?"

"Hell, no," she said. "Lacy was seventeen goin' on sixteen. She still had a lot of growin' up to do."

"As opposed to you?"

She looked me up and down and said, "So you're a private eye, huh?"

"Uh huh," I said. "So, what do you think, Angelica? Did Lacy leave on her own, or was she taken?"

"Taken?" she asked. "You mean, like Liam Neeson taken?"

"I mean like kidnapped."

"I don't see how anyone could've come into our room and kidnapped her without wakin' me up," she said.

"But you overslept the next mornin', didn't you?"

"Well...yeah." She folded her arms across her chest. "So?"

"Did you drink the night before?"

"Drink?"

"Anythin'," I said. "Could someone have slipped you a mickey?"

She looked totally confused.

"A mickey?"

"A drug," I said. "A roofie. Could someone have given you somethin'?"

"I guess so," she said. "I mean...we all ate in the cafeteria."

"Did everyone oversleep that mornin'?" I asked.

"I dunno...I guess so."

"I'll ask Mrs. Fenster," I said. "Did Lacy ever talk about a boy named Tommy?"

"She didn't talk about boys," she said. "We didn't talk about boys together. We were roommates, not friends."

"Well," I said, "if you can think of anythin' she might've said that could help, let me know." I handed her one of my cards.

"Headstone," she said. "Cool." She looked up at me. "Before we leave here, I'm really good at blowjobs." She mimed one, using her tongue on the inside of her cheek. "Want one?"

TWENTY-NINE

When Angelica left the office and Mrs. Fenster came back in we sat back down in our previous positions. Only I wasn't in my previous state of mind.

"Mrs. Fenster," I said, "I need you to stop jerkin' my chain."

"I'm sorry?"

"Stop fuckin' with me," I added. "Is that plainer?"

She stood up stiffly and pointed at the door.

"I think you better leave!"

"This idea you have that these students are all good little catholic girls who love it here is bunk," I told her. "You need to start givin' me some honest answers."

"I don't know what—"

"Your little Angelica, who just slouched out of here, offered me a blowjob."

She fell back into her chair with a stricken look on her face.

"What?"

"She said she was real good at it."

"Omigod!"

"Yeah," I said. "I'm wonderin' how many of the other girls would make the same offer?"

"Omi—"

"Look," I said, cutting her off, "let's stop the shocked act. I need some honest answers."

118

She stared at me, glassy-eyed, and asked, "What do you want to know?"

"The morning that you noticed Lacy was gone," I said, "did everyone oversleep?"

"As a matter of fact, yes," she said.

"So could everyone have been doped by somethin' put in the food or drink the night before?"

"Well, everyone ate in the cafeteria, so...oh, wait."

"What is it?"

"Lacy," she said, "she didn't eat or drink anything."

"What?"

"She complained she didn't feel good and went to her room," Mrs. Fenster said.

I hadn't expected that. Had Lacy given the entire school a mickey so she could just walk out the next morning?

"Lacy wasn't such a good girl, was she?" I asked.

"Well—"

"I looked at the folder when you left the room."

"That's privileged—"

"I figured you left it there deliberately for me to see."

She firmed her jaw, took off her glasses and rubbed her eyes. Without the specs she looked younger, softer. I had originally figured her for around fortysomething, but now I was thinking late thirties.

"Mrs. Fenster, how long have you been headmistress?"

"Only about four years."

"And did you go to this school when you were a teenager?"

"I did," she said, "and it was a wonderful place, then."

"But you were a good girl, weren't you?"

"I was, yes."

"And there were bad girls, too, right?"

"Yes, but I didn't...associate with them."

"I'm thinkin' you don't know how to handle them now any better than you did when you were a student."

"Well...they did tend to...intimidate me."

"Back then?"

"Yes."

"And they still do?"

She looked ashamed.

"Yes." She put her glasses back on, cleared her throat and squared her shoulders. "What are you thinking, Mr. Headston?"

"I was thinking that somebody could've dosed you all the night before so you'd oversleep," I said. "But it never occurred to me that the person who did it could be Lacy. I assume you have a science lab?"

"Yes, we do."

"I suppose she could've got somethin' from there to use," I said.

"I can ask our science teacher."

"That's good," I said. "Meanwhile, I'd like to talk to the dorm supervisor."

"I'll have her brought in."

"Thank you."

She stood up, hesitated, then said, "I'm sorry—"

"Never mind," I said. "Let's just cooperate with each other and see if we can figure out what happened."

THIRTY

The dorm supervisor was a senior named Melissa Thurber, a senior. She seemed more mature than her eighteen years. Mrs. Fenster told me she had been named dorm supervisor because she was mature, and very responsible.

As they entered the room Mrs. Fenster introduced us, and then left us alone.

"Did Mrs. Fenster tell you why you're here, Melissa?"

"Yes, sir," she said. "It's about Lacy Jonkowski."

"Have a seat, please," I invited. I had taken Mrs. Fenster's chair behind her desk, so Melissa sat across from me. She was a tall girl with a plain face, long blond hair. However, she knew how to use make-up, and managed to make herself almost pretty with it. The skirt she wore was tight, but of tasteful length. She was going to go far in life.

"Melissa, what can you tell me about Lacy?" I asked.

"Not much," she said. "I'm a senior, she's a junior. We don't really socialize."

"But you're the dorm supervisor in her dorm," I said. "Doesn't that mean you...interact?"

"Usually," she said, "I interact with girls when they need to be reminded, Mr. Headston."

"And how often was that necessary with Lacy?"

"Several times, actually."

"For what?"

"For sneaking a boy into her room."

"Didn't she have a roommate?"

"Yes," Melissa said, "a roommate who looked the other way."

"And did she get reported?"

"Expelled."

"Really?" I asked. "The girl who looked the other way was expelled, but Lacy wasn't?"

"I didn't get it either," Melissa said. She crossed her long legs and seemed very relaxed, but puzzled. "But it's not my call, is it?"

"What is your call?" I asked.

"Reporting them when they do something they shouldn't be doing," she said, "which is what I did."

I frowned.

"I thought Angelica Rogers was Lacy's roommate."

"She is now," Melissa said. "Her previous roommate was expelled."

"Okay," I said, "so what happened the night before Lacy disappeared?"

"She didn't disappear," Melissa said. "She ran off."

"Are you certain of that?"

"Of course I am," she said. "She went off with that boy, Tommy O."

"Tommy O?"

"Oronotti," she said, "but he likes to be called Tommy O. He thinks he's Mafia material."

"And you think she's gone off with him willingly?"

"Yes, I do," she said.

"Why?" I asked.

"Excuse me? Why what?"

"Why do you think she went with him willingly? What's her reason?"

"Well, for attention, of course," she answered. "You're here because her mother or father hired you, aren't you?"

"That's right."

"Well, there you go, then," she said. "Attention."

"So you don't think she's...in love?"

"With Tommy Oronotti?" She blew some air out of her mouth, making a rude noise. "No!"

"But isn't he the boy she sneaked up to her room?"

"One of them."

That surprised me.

"There were others?"

"Well, if you must know," Melissa said, "that girl's a slut."

I did need to know that, but it wasn't going to make her father very happy.

When Mrs. Fenster came back in and excused Melissa we changed places. She sat behind her desk, and I sat where Melissa had been.

"Was Melissa helpful?" she asked.

"Very," I said.

"She didn't uh..."

"...offer me a blowjob. No."

She looked relieved.

"She told me Lacy was a slut."

"Well..."

"Was she?"

"Well..."

"Mrs. Fenster—"

"Could you call me Helen, please?" she asked. "Fenster makes me sound so...fuddy-duddy."

"All right, Helen...I understand you might not want to refer to one of your students as 'slutty,' but...what would you call it?"

"Precocious?"

"Promiscuous?" I substituted.

"Possibly."

"And I understand she'd been caught more than once with a boy in her room."

"Yes."

"And always a different boy?"

"For a while," she said, "until she met Tommy."

"And I understand her previous roommate was expelled for, uh, looking the other way, but Lacy wasn't expelled, and she was the one with the boy in her room. Why is that? Why the girl who looked away and not the girl guilty of the infraction?"

"We had no choice with Emily—the roommate," Helen Fenster said. "I had to let her go."

"And why not Lacy?"

"Well...Lacy's father is quite generous with the school. If I expelled her I'd have a lot of explaining to do to the school board."

"Wait," I said, "you know who Lacy's father is?"

"Well, no, just that he's, well, generous."

"But the board knows who he is?"

"Oh, I'm sure."

That shed a bit of new light on things.

THIRTY-ONE

Sugar had told me that no one knew Lacy was his daughter. Now I heard from Helen Fenster that the school board knew. I had to find out how many of them there were, and how many of them knew. I only had Melissa's word that Lacy had gone off willingly. Sugar being Sugar, I was still going to assume she'd been taken, until I found out otherwise.

"Helen," I said, "I'm going to need the names and contact information for everyone on the school board. How many members are there?"

"Five," she said. "You can pick it up from my assistant on the way out. Is there anything else I can do for you, Mr. Headston?"

"Not right now," I said, standing. "I've still got some other leads to follow up, but I'll check back with you if I need anything else."

I picked the list up from her assistant and headed out.

My next stop was Mary-Ann Jonkowski.

I took the train from Manhattan to Brooklyn, and a cab to Mary-Ann's address. I had an odd case of nerves as I walked up to the front door of her split-level ranch that had been top of the line in the sixties. In the eighties it had been weathered, and Mary-Ann was top of the line. Now the house was dilapidated, and I was wondering if Mary-Ann was, too? Thirty-four years can do a lot of damage. I'm living proof.

I rang the doorbell and waited. When the door opened I was transported back in time. Mary-Ann Jonkowski still looked like Mary-Ann Jonkowski, just with some additional lines and wrinkles, none of which were as debilitating as the lines and wrinkles on her house.

"Yes?"

"Hi, Mary-Ann," I said.

She frowned.

"Do I know you?"

"You did about thirty-four years ago, in Canarsie High School."

She studied me for a full minute, and then her face brightened.

"Johnny Headstone!"

"Right," I said. "I thought you might remember my face, but not my name."

"Naw, your face is...uh, it's your eyes."

"Oh."

"What can I do for you?" She folded her arms. It seemed fairly obvious she wasn't going to invite me in. "You're not here about a reunion, because you never came."

"No," I said, "I'm here about Lacy."

"Who?"

"Lacy, your daughter."

"I don't understand," she said, "I have two sons, and neither of them is named Lacy."

"No, I mean your daughter, the seventeen-year-old who's missing?"

She shook her head and looked blank.

"Who told you I have a seventeen-year-old daughter?"

"Well...Dominick Garbanzo told me."

"That douche bag!" she snapped. "What makes him think I have a daughter?"

"He, uh, said it was you and he who had the daughter," I told her.

"What?"

"He said you hooked up at a reunion about eighteen years ago. Just one drunken night."

"Get this straight, buster," she said, pointing her forefinger at me. "I have never slept with Sugar Garbanzo. I'd have to be so drunk I was unconscious! If my husband was home I'd have him kick your ass."

"And you don't have a daughter."

"No!" she shouted. "Now go away!" She started to close the door, then stopped and said, "And come to a reunion some time." Then slammed it.

Oh Sugar, Sugar...

When I got back to the office Ally said excitedly, "Jesus, the police have been callin' you."

"What about?"

"Murder."

"Who's dead?"

"You know that Pennyworth case you had a while back?"

"You mean it finally happened?" I asked. "Somebody killed him?"

"Somebody got killed, all r ght," she said, "but it wasn't the husband. It was the wife. Your old girlfriend is dead!"

THIRTY-TWO

Constance Pennyworth was not only dead, she had been murdered.

I had worked with NYPD Detectives Stokes and Leon a short while ago, and now that Constance Pennyworth was dead, someone had told them of my involvement with the family.

After Ally gave me the message that they wanted to see me I went to their office at One Police Plaza and asked for Detective Leon or Detective Stokes. Leon came out, a fortyish man with a thickening middle, and took me back to an interrogation room.

"Couldn't we have done this at your desk?" I asked.

"We're investigating a homicide, Mr. Headston," he said. "We'll do it by the numbers, if you don't mind."

"So am I a suspect, or simply a person of interest?"

"Right now you're just somebody who might be able to shed some light on a few things."

"Does that mean I get coffee?"

As if on cue the door opened and his partner, Stokes, came in. He was ten years younger than Leon, and in better shape. He was carrying three containers of coffee.

"Brought it in from outside," he announced, setting one down in front of me. "Our in-house brew is swill."

"Thanks."

He placed one next to his partner's elbow, then stepped back and leaned against a wall with his. They taught this technique in the academy, one seated, one standing.

"Tell us about your involvement with the Pennyworth family," Leon said.

I hesitated, wondering how far I should go back. Then I reasoned that he had asked about the Pennyworth family. No point in me going all the way back to when Constance Pennyworth was Carla Balducci.

So I told them about Constance Pennyworth hiring me to find out who was threatening her husband, how it turned out that someone might have been threatening the entire family, and how in the end I decided I was being played, and withdrew from the case.

"What made you think you were being played?"

I couldn't tell him that Carla/Constance had made a fool out of me once, before, so I said, "Nothing was making sense. It all stated to sound to me like a family squabble, with the new young wife and the daughters all scrambling for an inheritance when the old man died."

"Or was killed," Leon said.

"Yes."

"And you say the daughters thought they were in danger, too?"

"One did," I said, "the young one, Sarah."

"And who did she think was a threat to her?"

"Well, she said her husband."

"Piers."

"Right."

"But?"

"He came to New York, seemed concerned about her. Like I said, nothing was making sense to me."

"And nobody ever said anything about the wife, Constance, being in danger?"

"No," I said, "she was the one who brought me in, and apparently the only one who wasn't in danger."

"And yet she's the one who's been murdered," Leon told me.

"That's what my secretary said," I answered. "How was she killed? Where?"

"She and her husband were staying at the Four Seasons. He went to a meeting, and found her when he came back. She'd been strangled."

"Break-in?" I asked.

"Could've been," Leon said, "but it's early, yet."

"When did she hire you?" Stokes asked.

"About three months ago," I said. "And at the time, they were staying at the Four Seasons. I got the impression it was their regular place when they were in town."

"And when they weren't in town?" Leon asked. "Where did they live?"

"One of their other homes," I said.

"Do you know where those are?"

"Maine, California and France."

Stokes whistled.

"And the attempts, or accidents, with her husband, they happened where?"

"Maine, France, and upstate New York."

"And did you check out those locations?"

"I never got around to it. I had talked to them all here in Manhattan, and decided I was being played."

"And you never talked to the police about it?"

"Not here," I said, "not you guys and, like I said, I hadn't gone on location, yet. If I'd pursued the case I would've talked to the locals in all those places."

"That would've entailed a lot of travel."

"Yes, it would."

"What were you chargin' her for all this?"

"My usual fee," I said. "She would've covered my travel expenses."

"You could've strung her along for a while," Stokes said. "Why quit?"

"I don't do business that way," I said.

"Okay, back to the present," Leon said. "Do you have any idea who might've killed Mrs. Pennyworth, if it wasn't a break-in?"

"No."

"You said the daughters didn't like her."

"Would they have strangled her?" I asked. "That's not usually a woman's first go to method."

"They could've had it done," he said. "Maybe one of the husbands."

"Maybe."

"Which one?" Stokes asked, "Pick one you think might've done it."

I figured Sarah's Piers would be the most likely one, but I didn't want to say that.

"Guys, I don't know," I said. "All I can say is, that family was kind of mixed-up, and the husbands didn't seem to fit in."

Leon looked over at Stokes, who just raised his eyebrows.

"All right, Mr. Headston," Leon said, standing up. "You can go. But we might need to talk to you again."

"I'm always available, Detective," I said, rising.

As I passed him on the way to the door Stokes said, "And if you happen to think of anything that might be helpful, please give us a call."

"I will. And do you have any objection to my going to see Mr. Pennyworth?"

"What for?"

"Just to pay my respects," I said.

"Not to drum up business?" Leon asked.

"What kind of business?" I asked. "This is a murder. That's your bailiwick, not mine."

"You'd do well to remember that," Leon said. "Go ahead and pay your respects."

"Is he still at the Four Seasons?" I asked.

"As far as we know."

I nodded and said, "Detectives."

"Mr. Headston," Leon said. "Thanks for comin' down."

* * *

Outside the building I took out my cell and called Ally.

"Any calls?" I asked.

"No. Are you comin' back here?"

"I'm going to the Four Seasons to see Alan Pennyworth. Don't wait for me, just close up and go on home when you're ready, Ally."

"You got it, boss."

I broke the connection and headed for the subway.

THIRTY-THREE

Pennyworth was not in the same room he had occupied the last time I saw him, but that might have been because his wife was killed there, and he moved.

I was surprised when I knocked and the door was opened by his oldest daughter, Angela.

"Mr. Headston," she said. "I'm not sure why you're here."

"I heard," I said. "I wanted to pay my respects to your father."

"Come in, then," she said, backing away.

I entered, closed the door and followed her. Pennyworth was sitting on a large, plush Four Seasons sofa, holding a drink. There were three other people in the room, none of whom I knew.

"Dad," Angela said, "you remember Mr. Headston."

"Headston," he said, and then looked up at me. Recognition dawned. "Headston!" he said, again. "Everybody out, please!"

"Mr. Pennyworth—" one grey-haired man said.

"Out, William!" Pennyworth said. "No business today! Angela, you stay."

William and the two other men in expensive suits filed out. I was thinking, lawyers.

"Goddamned lawyers!" he snapped.

"Now Dad—"

"Angela, get Mr. Headston a drink, please,"

"Bourbon?" she asked, looking at me.

"Please."

"Have a seat, Mr. Headston," Pennyworth said. "I'm glad you're here."

I sat in an armchair that matched the sofa. I was afraid I'd never want to get up.

"When did it happen?" I asked.

"Last night," he said. "I still...haven't accepted it."

Angela came over and handed me a tumbler of bourbon. Then she backed off with her own drink and remained standing.

"I was at meetings all day. Constance told me she'd be shopping. When I came back last night she was...lying there. Her pearls were...scattered around her."

"In this suite?" I asked.

"No, we were in another one...one floor up."

"What did you do?"

"I called the police."

"Did you call anyone else?"

"I called Angela," he said, "and my lawyer, Winston Chase. He was just here."

"Why him?"

He hesitated, then said, "You know, I'm not sure. I mean, whenever anything went wrong over the past forty years, I'd call him. It was just...instinct."

"I see."

"Mr. Headston," he said, "I want to hire you."

"To do what?"

"What else? Find out who killed my wife."

"That's a police matter, Mr. Pennyworth," I said. "I can't work an active homicide. I'd lose my license." Again.

"Correct me if I'm wrong," he said. "It's up to the police to arrest the guilty party."

"That's correct."

"So what if you discovered who it was, and told them?" Pennyworth asked. "I'm not asking you to arrest anybody."

I knew this could be a slippery slope.

"I'll tell you what I'll do," Pennyworth went on. "I'll put you on staff. Technically, you'll be working for me, and for my lawyer, Winston."

"Is he a criminal lawyer?"

"Not primarily, but he has worked criminal cases when necessary."

"I still wouldn't be able to work an active homicide case."

"Then let's call it something else," he said. "Let's say you're investigating my wife's life, to see if she was cheating. And, in the course of that investigation, if you find the killer, you'll give him to the police. Can they object to that?"

"Let's ask your lawyer," I suggested.

"Good idea."

"Dad," Angela said, "is this wise?"

He looked at her.

"What do you propose I do?"

"Leave it to the police," she said. "It may have just been a break-in."

"Three months ago," Pennyworth said, "somebody was trying to kill me. Now Constance is dead. Do you think that's a coincidence?"

"Well, no, but—"

"Let me finish with Mr. Headston," Pennyworth said, turning his attention back to me. "I'll put you on salary, say...two hundred thousand a year? All benefits. Then you can get together with Winston—"

"I don't think that's going to work, Mr. Pennyworth," I said, not believing the words that were coming out of my own mouth. Turning down two hundred thou a year? Was I crazy?

"Why not?"

"That would make it look like you bought me," I said. "But I'll talk to your lawyer and we'll work out a fee schedule. As long as he's done criminal work, I think I can be covered by working for him."

"Then you'll do it?" he asked. "You'll find out who killed her?"

"I'll look into it and see what I can find," I said. "But if the cops come after me, I'll have to back off, lawyer or no."

"I'll leave that up to you," he said.

I looked at Angela.

"Did you see Constance yesterday?"

"No."

I looked at Pennyworth.

"Did anyone see her?"

"Someone must have."

"I mean, anyone in the family?"

"I don't think so."

"Where's Sarah?"

"Back home in Vermont," Angela said.

"And her husband?"

"I don't know," she said. "They split up."

"When?"

"About two months ago."

"And you and Harrison?"

"Still together," she said.

I looked at Pennyworth.

"Sir, have there been any changes to your will since last we spoke?"

"Some," he said. "My lawyer can go over that with you."

"Where's his office?"

"On Madison Avenue, up in the sixties."

That was a high rent district.

"Does he have a one-man operation?"

"It's a firm," Pennyworth said, "but his name is one of them on the door."

"Do his partners work for you?"

"We're exclusive."

"Who were the other two men who were here when I entered?"

"Lackies, yes men. They should be of no concern to you."

"When you made him leave where would he have gone?" I asked. "Back to his office?"

"The bar," Angela said. "Downstairs."

"I can call and have him come back up," Pennyworth offered.

"Call him," I suggested, getting to my feet, "but tell him I'm coming down."

THIRTY-FOUR

I told Pennyworth I'd be back after I talked with his lawyer. I was going to have more questions.

"Do I have to stay?" Angela asked.

"Not as long as I can find you."

"I'll be home."

"Fine."

Pennyworth asked me to send the yes-men back up when I got downstairs.

I entered the hotel bar and saw the three men seated at a small round table, each with a drink in front of him. The lawyer, Winston Chase, was just setting down his cell phone. He stood when he saw me coming.

"Mr. Headston," he said, extending his hand, "Winston Chase."

"Good to meet you," I said, shaking his hand. I looked at the two younger men. "Mr. Pennyworth would like you two upstairs."

"Oh, yes, that's right," Chase said. "He mentioned that on the phone just now." He looked at them. "Go!"

The two men scurried out.

"Have a seat, Mr. Headston," Chase said. "Drink?"

I hadn't finished the drink up in the suite, so I figured, why not?

"Bourbon, neat," I said.

He called a black skirted waitress over and said, "Bourbon, neat. Put it on Mr. Pennyworth's room."

The waitress looked at me.

"King's County or Woodford Reserve, sir?"

"I might as well stay local," I said. "I'll have the Kings County." Even though it came from Brooklyn, it was easily fifty bucks a bottle. And since it was going on Pennyworth's bill, why not?

"I saw you were on the phone when I came in," I said. "Did Mr. Pennyworth tell you what he wants from me?"

"Yes," he said, "and from me. I'll give you a check that will put you under retainer to my firm, Chase, Meyer and Walcott."

I had heard of the firm, but didn't know they took on any criminal cases.

"How much criminal work do you do, Mr. Chase?"

"Not much," he said, "but when the firm does get a criminal case, it comes to me."

He handed me one of his cards, with the firm's name, logo and Madison Avenue address.

"Well," I said, "if the cops catch on that I'm investigating, I may be calling you."

"My cell number is on there," Chase said. "If you need me, I'll be there."

"That's comforting."

"Just don't tell anyone that you're investigating a murder," he suggested. "Say you were hired to look into Mrs. Pennyworth's last hours."

"That's probably the best way to go," I agreed. "Tell me, did you see Constance yesterday?"

"No, I didn't."

"How long have she and Mr. Pennyworth been in town?"

"A week," he said. "Alan and I had a lot of business to attend to."

"So Constance was left alone a lot?"

139

"Yes," Chase said. "Usually until evening."

"Do you know if she was...seeing anyone?"

"You mean...cheating on Alan?"

"Yes, that's what I mean."

Chase didn't answer right away. The waitress came with my bourbon and I nodded my thanks. I sipped and went right to heaven.

"What makes you ask that?" Chase asked.

"It's a common question when a husband or wife is killed," I said.

"They've been married twelve years, and were devoted to each other all that time."

"Are you sure?"

"Do you have some reason to think otherwise?"

"Like I said," I replied, "common question."

"You know," Chase said, "we didn't meet three months ago when Constance hired you, but I've always wondered...why you?"

"Why not me?"

"Please, don't get me wrong," Chase said. "I don't mean to insult you, but I could've gotten Constance any one of a number of reputable private detectives. I always wondered why she chose you. Did you and she know each other?"

"That's very good, Mr. Chase," I said. "Yes, Constance and I knew each other, years ago."

"Where?"

"Here, in New York," I said. "But I hadn't seen her in many years."

"And yet she called you for help."

"Hired me," I said. "She knew I was good at my job."

"You know," Chase said, "I warned Alan not to marry her."

"Why?"

"I thought she was a gold digger," he said. "Why else would she marry a man twenty years older than she was?"

"Maybe she loved him."

"Could be," he said. "They lasted twelve years, although I always wondered..."

"Wondered what?"

"If Alan was living too long to suit her," Chase said. "I mean, twelve years, that's a long time to wait for someone to die so you can inherit. Maybe she's the one who was trying to kill him."

"If that was the case, why hire me?"

He shrugged.

"To throw suspicion off herself when he turned up dead?"

"And then she's the one who shows up dead," I said.

"I know," he said. "It doesn't make any sense."

"If you thought she was trying to kill your employer—"

"Alan is more than my employer, he's my friend. Has been for years."

"Then that gives you a motive to kill Constance, doesn't it?"

"What?" He looked shocked.

"Sure. To save your friend."

"My friend loved his wife," Chase said, "and after twelve years, I'd be a fool to do anything. And I resent the implication."

"It was more than an implication," I said, "it was a suggestion, but you handled it quite well."

"You were testing me?"

"I was doing what I do, Mr. Chase," I said. "I ask questions. Which reminds me, I still have some for Mr. Pennyworth."

"Well, not today, please," Chase said. "I'm trying to get him to take this situation in. And we still have a lot of arrangements to make."

"Well, I doubt the coroner will be releasing the body for some time," I said.

"I understand that." He took out a checkbook, leaned forward on the table in front of us and wrote a check that he signed with a flourish. Then he tore it off and held it out to me.

"You're now on a retainer," he said. "Go ahead and ask

your questions."

I made a concerted effort to fold the check and put it in my pocket without looking at it. Then I picked up my bourbon and finished it.

I stood up to leave, but hesitated.

"Like you told Constance, you have a lot of investigators on your staff and in your directory," I said. "Why me?"

"Alan wants you," he said. "That's good enough for me. So keep my card on you and call if you need me."

"I'll be in touch," I promised.

THIRTY-FIVE

I went back to the office to collect myself.

"Are you all right?" Ally asked, as I entered.

"I thought you were going home."

"I wanted to make sure you were all right," she said. "After all, you knew her."

"I never knew her at all," I told her.

"Still...what happened?"

Briefly, I told her what I did know, that someone had gotten into the Pennyworth suite and strangled Constance.

"How'd they get in?"

"I don't know, yet," I said. "I have a lot of questions to ask, but I wanted to come back here first and...sit."

"Did the husband hire you?"

"Technically, the lawyer hired me, but yeah, I'm hired."

"To do what? You're always tellin' me you can't work on an active police case. Aren't you gonna get into trouble, workin' on a murder?"

"I'm not going to work the murder," I said. "I'm going to investigate the last hours of her life and see what she was doing."

"That's sneaky," she said. "Is it gonna work?"

"I don't know," I said. "I guess I'll find out when Detectives Leon and Stokes come after me. Meanwhile...go on home, Ally. Tomorrow we'll get started."

"We?"

"I've got that other case, too, the missing girl, and I may have some things for you to do."

"Well, all right!" she said. "I get out of the office?"

"Maybe," I said. "Don't get your hopes up. I already know my client lied to me."

"That Sugar guy?"

"Yeah, my old friend is telling me lies," I said. "Which should be no surprise, knowing Sugar."

"Okay, okay," she said, waving her arms, "I won't get my hopes up, but I'll be ready." She rubbed her hands over her bare tattooed arms. "I'll cover my tats tomorrow."

"Good-night, Ally."

"'night, boss." She surprised me by coming up to and putting her arms around me. "I'm sorry about your friend."

She left, and I stood there a minute, wondering if I could even think of Constance/Carla as my friend.

I made sure the outer door was locked, then went in and sat at my desk. I had left Carla behind, but now that she was dead as "Constance" she was back. But even before I started working on her "last hours" I had to deal with the fact that Sugar Garbanzo had lied to me. Did he think I wouldn't find out about that? That Mary-Ann Jonkowski wouldn't tell me she'd never heard of a girl named Lacy? What was Sugar thinking?

THIRTY-SIX

I had a lot to do.

I was going to have to confront Sugar at some point about lying to me that Mary-Ann was Lacy's mother. But I thought I should hear from the school board first and find out what they knew about Lacy's parents.

At the same time, I had to get over to the Four Seasons and question the staff about Constance's movements the day she was killed. That meant talking to desk staff, maids, bellboys, valets, the doorman, and possibly wait staff and bartenders. That was time consuming, so I decided to leave the school board members to Ally.

When I got to the office she was there, seated at her desk. She was wearing a blouse with three-quarter sleeves that covered most of her tats, but I saw a jacket hanging on the back of her chair. She was ready, but she was going to be disappointed when I told her what I wanted her to do.

"Good-mornin', boss," she said, pointing to a bag on her desk. "I brought the bagels this mornin'."

"I appreciate that," I said, wasting no time finding a sesame seed in the bag and plucking it out.

"There's a container of coffee on your desk," she said.

I was hoping she wouldn't take the coffee and bagel back when I explained my plan to her.

"When do we get started?" she asked.

"Let me get my coffee," I said. I went into my office, took the lid off the container and turned to see that she had followed me in.

"So?"

"I've got a list of the board members at the school Lacy disappeared from." I stopped right there, as I recalled that Lacy was enrolled as Lacy "Jonkowski."

"What is it?" she asked.

"Nothing," I said. "Something just occurred to me. But it doesn't change what I want you to do."

"Interview the board members?"

"Yes. By phone."

"Noooo!"

"It'll be easier that way," I said, "not as time consuming. And I just have a few questions for each. I want you to find out what they know about Lacy's parents."

"You wanna know who they are, and if they know who Sugar Garbanzo really is, right?"

"Right."

"You know I could really dig into it in person, don't ya?" she demanded.

"Look," I said, "if you can't get any of them on the phone, that'll be the next step. But for now do it my way, okay?"

She sighed and said, "Yeah, okay."

"Good girl."

"Drink your coffee."

She went back to her desk.

I ate my bagel, washed it down with the coffee, then walked out and put the list of names, addresses and phone numbers down on her desk.

"Where're you gonna be if I need you?" she asked.

"I'll be at the Four Seasons, probably most of the day," I said. "There are a lot of people to talk to, there."

"Go," she said, "I've gotta get busy." She picked up her cell phone, preferring it to the office landline.

I left her to it.

The Four Seasons was definitely far out of my league, but I wore my best suit to try to fit in.

I checked in first with management, so they'd know I was on the premises. I didn't need to have my investigation interrupted by hotel security. When I told the manager I was working for Alan Pennyworth, his attitude changed and he promised me full cooperation.

I started with the front desk staff, to see if any of them had seen Mrs. Pennyworth during the day. One of them, a young girl in her twenties, said she saw Constance go out in the morning, after her husband had left.

"Why'd you notice her?" I asked.

"Because she's in her fifties and she's beautiful," the girl said. "I hope I can look that good when I'm old."

"How was she dressed when you saw her?"

"Um, very tastefully."

"What I mean is," I said, "do you think she was dressed to... meet someone?"

"Someone?"

"A man."

"Oh, I see," she said. "Well, she was wearing a jacket and skirt, and her great legs were showing...I guess she could've been. Her make-up was perfect..."

"But?" I asked, because I heard the unspoken "but" in her tone.

"But it was always perfect," she said. "I wish I could've gotten lessons."

She was a pretty girl who looked to be wearing very little in the way of make-up, but I didn't comment.

I looked at the name tag on her vest.

"Vicki," I said, "I'll need to know who the maid is who cleaned the Pennyworth suite."

"There are a couple," she said. "I can write their names down for you."

"Thank you. And where would I find them?"

"They should probably be on that floor now," she told me.

"And are there certain bellmen, or room service staff, that service that floor?"

"I'll write that down for you, as well," she said.

"You're being a big help. Thank you."

It took her a few minutes to find all the names and write them. I was able to talk to two bellmen and the doorman over the next half hour. The bellmen hadn't seen her, but the doorman had...

THIRTY-SEVEN

"I got her a cab," he said. "She tipped generously."

"Did you hear where she was going?" I asked.

"Well, yeah," he said. "She told me, and I told the driver. She was going to Bergdorf's."

Bergdorf-Goodman was on Fifth Avenue and Fifty-Seventh Street, which meant it was close to the Plaza Hotel. There were also some smaller hotels in the area. I'd have to check them all to see if Constance met anyone there.

Why did I think she might have been cheating? Because when I met her she was cheating with me.

"Did you see her return?"

"No," he said, "I must've been off duty when she came back. You'd have to check with my relief. He should be here at five."

"Thanks."

Next came the maids. I found both of them on the Pennyworth floor, and asked them the same question.

"Did you ever find anything in the room that might lead you to believe that Mrs. Pennyworth was being unfaithful?"

The Jamaican maid said, "What woman would be foolish enough to use her husband's suite to cheat on him? No, I see nothin'."

The Latina maid said, "I see nothin', but I would not be surprised."

"Why's that?" I asked.

"Husband old, wife younger," she said, and shrugged, as if that told the whole story.

"Okay, thank you."

Room service told me they had only ever seen Constance alone, or with her husband, when they delivered food to the suite. In almost every case, though, the two room service guys smiled and said Constance was always in a negligee.

"And lookin' pretty damn good for a woman her age," the older one said.

The younger one said, "She was always lookin' hot."

"She ever flirt with you if she was alone when you got there?" I asked the younger one.

"All the time," he said, "but I like my job, and she wasn't that hot. Now, Mrs. Richards, one floor down…"

The regular bellman said they had no dealings with her except to bring the luggage up when the couple arrived, and take the luggage down when they were checking out.

By the time I finished with the desk staff, the doormen—the night guy only ever took her out of a cab, never put her in one—the bellman and the maids, I had no indication that Constance had brought any lovers to the hotel.

That left only the bartenders and waitresses in the bar…

"Martinis," the bartender said.

"Every time?" I asked.

"Even when she ordered a drink to be brought up to her room," he said. "A martini—gin."

"Have you ever brought a drink to her room yourself?" I asked.

"No," he said, "it's my job to make it, not deliver it. But I gotta tell you, even though she's twenty years older than me, I wouldn't have minded."

"Have you ever seen her in here with a man other than her husband?" I asked.

"Well, yes."

"Do you know who he was?"

"The lawyer, the fella you were in here with yesterday."

"Mr. Chase?"

"Is that his name? Yes, him."

"Often?"

"No," he said, "just once or twice during their visits."

The manager had already told me that the Pennyworths would come to town for a week or two.

I talked with the waitress next, the same one who had served me my bourbon the day before.

"Oh sure," she said, "I've served her. Gin martini, right?"

"That's right. Have you seen her in here with men?"

"Sometimes alone," the girl said, "sometimes with her husband, once or twice with the lawyer, the man you were sittin' with yesterday."

"No one else?" I asked. "Another woman, maybe?"

"No," she said, "not during my shift, but maybe the bartender—"

"This one pretty much tells the same tale you do," I said.

"If you come back tomorrow at noon," she said, "there'll be another waitress and another bartender. You could ask them."

"I think I'll do that," I said. "Thanks, Vicki."

"Always glad to help the police," she said.

"Oh, I'm not the police," I was quick to correct. I had to make sure that I, at no time, made anyone think I was the police. "I'm a private detective."

"Oh!" she said. "Well, that's even more exciting!" She turned to go back to the bar, then whirled around and asked, "Can I get you somethin'?"

"I'd like a glass of water."

"Comin' up."

I sat at one of the small tables and she came trotting over with a tall glass of water.

"I put ice in it for you."

"Thanks, Vicki."

She turned and went back to the bar.

I sipped the water and considered my next move. At that moment, my cell rang.

"Johnny, I got three of them," Ally said. "If you want me to get the other two I'll have to go and see them."

"What did the three say?"

"They never heard of Mary-Ann Jonkowski, but they do know that Mr. Garbanzo is Lacy's father."

"And do they know what Sugar does for a living?"

"Accordin' to all three he's a businessman."

This didn't help me figure out why Sugar had lied about Mary-Ann, knowing that I'd go and see her and find out.

"Should I go interview the other two?"

"No," I said, "that won't be necessary. They'll just tell you the same thing,"

"Damn!" she swore. "So I'm stuck in the office."

I thought about the waitress and bartender who would be in the Four Seasons bar the next afternoon.

"Not necessarily," I said.

"Huh?"

"How would you like to have a drink at the Four Seasons?"

THIRTY-EIGHT

The next day I left it to Ally to go to the Four Seasons and talk to the other bartender and waitress. I called Sugar and arranged to meet him at the same restaurant in Little Italy. He was sitting at the same table, already working on an antipasto plate.

"I was hungry, so I ordered," he told me as I sat. "You're gettin' baked ziti today."

"That's fine."

"I'm gettin' mussels," he said. "You don't know what you're missin', not eatin' seafood."

He was wearing another track suit, only this one was purple with red striping.

There was a bottle of Peroni on the table already, so I grabbed it and drank it. I was about to call Sugar Garbonzo a liar. The last time I did that he threw me a beating in the school yard.

"Whataya got for me, Johnny?" he asked, around a mouthful of pepperoni.

"Well, Sugar," I said, "I'd have a lot more if you hadn't lied to me."

He stopped chewing and stared at me.

"You talked to Mary-Ann?"

"I did."

"And she denied being Lacy's mother?"

153

"She did."

"I knew she would."

"Because she's not?"

"No," he said, "because she'd never wanna admit she slept with me."

"So you're telling me that Mary-Ann is the one lying."

"Yeah."

The waiter came with my ziti and Sugar's mussels.

"You want that last piece of prosciutto?" Sugar asked.

"No."

He snagged it and the waiter took the empty plate away.

"Who else did you talk to?"

"Mrs. Fenster, and some of the board members."

"Ah, Fenster," he said. "I'd like to bang that broad."

"Never mind that," I said, "to her and the board members, you're just a businessman."

"And I am."

He attacked his mussels. I had a bite of ziti, but I really wasn't there for lunch.

"Sugar, you're sending me mixed signals."

"How so?"

"You told me it's a secret you're her father."

"Right."

"But the school knows."

"But they don't know who I really am," he said, "or was. And they don't show their records to the student. Lacy doesn't know."

"And Mary-Ann doesn't know."

"Mary-Ann has a husband, and two other kids," he said. "She doesn't wanna know, and she doesn't want her husband to know."

"So before going to board at school did Lacy live with Mary-Ann and her husband?"

"Well, yeah."

"And who did the husband think was her father?"

He shrugged. "I don't know what she told him."

"Sugar—"

"Look, Johnny," Sugar said, cutting me off, "you're ruinin' my lunch. Never mind who the school thinks her father is, or who Mary-Ann's husband thinks he is, or why Mary-Ann's lyin' through her fat ass...just do what I'm payin' ya to do. Find the girl, bring 'er back. That's all I care about. That's all the school cares about, so that's all you should care about. In fact, you got any other cases?"

"I do have something—"

"Well, drop it," he said. "I'll pay you enough to cover your nut for a few months. How's that?"

"Sugar—"

"Eat your ziti," he said. "Lemme eat my mussels."

So we ate...

Sugar was lying, Mary-Ann might've been lying, I would've bet Fenster was lying about something. Why was I surprised? People lied all the time. Especially to the police and private detectives.

And Sugar was willing to pay me a lot of money to find the girl, whether it was his daughter or not. Why did that have to matter to me? Take the money and run, right?

Wrong. History told me when I had a fifty-fifty chance of making the right decision, I made the wrong one. But I couldn't help wonder what story the girl would tell if I found her.

This time Sugar ordered cannoli for dessert without checking with me first.

"Did you know," he asked, picking his up, "that cannoli is the plural, but the singular is cannolo?"

"No, I didn't know that."

"Only real Italians do," he said.

Well, come on, his last name was Garbanzo.

"So, whataya gonna do, Johnny?" he asked. "Find Lacy, or toss my money back in my fat face?"

Since I wasn't prepared to toss his money back I said, "I'll find her."

"Good. Do you need more money?"

"Not yet," I said. "I'll bill you when I'm done, Sugar."

"Good," he said, again. "Just use the address that was on the check."

"Thanks for lunch, Sugar."

"Johnny," he said, as I turned to leave, "leave Mary-Ann alone. She's a little…high strung."

"I'll do my best," I promised, and left.

THIRTY-NINE

Murder took precedence over a missing person.

Although, technically speaking, I wasn't investigating a murder. I was looking for what one woman had done the day of her murder, and what another woman—or girl—was doing now.

I left Sugar and took the subway uptown to St. Mary's. I had some more questions for Mrs. Fenster, and probably could've asked them on the phone, but I decided to do it in person.

I made my way through the hallways under the stares of the curious students. As I entered the outer office, Mrs. Fenster came out of her office. She stopped when she spotted me, and I had the feeling she wanted to duck back in.

"Mrs. Fenster," I said.

"Mr. Headston," she replied.

"Can I have a moment of your time?"

"Well, I was on my way to a meeting—"

"I won't take long," I promised. "Just a few more questions."

Mrs. Fenster looked at her secretary, who was watching us curiously, and then said, "Yes, all right, in my office."

I followed her into her office, where she closed the door and sat behind her desk.

"What can I do for you?"

"May I sit?"

She nodded and waved to a chair.

"Have you heard anything about Lacy?" I asked.

"No," she said. "I was going to ask you the same question."

"Nothing yet," I said. "But I need to know...have you ever met or spoken to Lacy's mother?"

"No."

"So you've only dealt with her father?"

"Well...no."

"Then who registered Lacy at your school?"

"This was three years ago, Mr. Headston," she said.

"But you must've had a meeting with an adult back then, somebody who came in with Lacy for an interview?"

"Yes."

"Then you remember who it was."

She hesitated, then said, "I do."

"Can you tell me who it was?" I asked. "That person might be able to help us."

"I can look it up."

"Please do."

She left the office and came back in with Lacy's file. It was the one I had perused, but I hadn't seen anything about who had registered her.

She sat, opened the folder, flipped through and then came out with a business card.

"It was a lawyer from this firm," she said, handing me the card.

I looked at the card and immediately recognized it. It was identical to the one in my wallet that I had received from Chase, Meyer and Walcott.

"And do you recall the name of the actual lawyer who was here?" I asked, handing the card back.

"Yes," she said, "it was Winston Chase, one of the partners."

"And he was representing Lacy's father?"

"Yes."

"During the course of a semester, don't the parents have to come in for meetings with teachers?"

"Usually."

"But not Lacy's?"

"Sometimes, we make...special..."

"Arrangements?" I asked. "Bend the rules?"

"There are parents who simply can't make the meetings," she said. "We try to...cooperate."

"And do such parents...has Lacy's father made donations to the school?"

"He's been...very generous, yes."

"Do you know if Lacy ever sees her father?"

"I...don't believe so."

"Does she even know who he is?"

"I don't know...I don't think so."

"Isn't it true you've been instructed never to tell her?"

"Well, yes..." She squirmed uncomfortably.

"Does your school board know about these special...circumstances?"

"Yes, they do."

"But the arrangements were made through you, is that right?"

"Yes."

"And does the money come to you?"

"No!" she snapped. "That's...insulting."

"I'm sorry," I said. "I didn't mean to insult you. Please forgive me."

She looked at her watch.

"Is there anything else?" she asked. "My meeting..."

"The boy, Tommy," I said, "have you ever met him?"

"No."

"Do you think any of the teachers ever have?"

"No," she said. "He just...sneaked into the dorm."

"So Melissa Thurber saw him when she caught them?"

"I assume so."

"And Lacy's roommate must've seen him."

"Yes."

"I'd like to talk with them, again."

"As I said, I have a meeting, but I'll have them brought in," she said, standing. "And considering what you told me last time about Angelica, I hope you don't mind if I have Miriam chaperone."

"Not at all."

"Just wait here, please."

She left the office and it seemed to me if she hadn't been wearing high heels, she would have run.

FORTY

Miriam came into the room and asked me in what order I'd like to see the girls. On the spot, I decided to see them together. When she brought them in Melissa smiled, but Angelica winked at me.

"No blowjob today, Angelica," I said, "so don't offer."

She looked shocked for effect and said, "What?"

"Don't act so innocent, Angelica," Melissa said. "You were seen shining the custodian's knob."

"Oh, Lord," Miriam said, turning red.

"Miriam, I think the girls can chaperone each other," I said, "and you can leave the door open."

"Thank you," she said, and hurried from the room.

"You're a bastard!" Angelica said to me, then turned to Melissa and said, "You're a bitch."

"And you're gonna be cleaning the bathrooms in the dorm," Melissa said, before turning to me. "What's on your mind, Mr. Private Eye?"

"You two," I said. "You're the ones I think can tell me how to find Tommy O."

"The kid Lacy snuck into the dorm?" Melissa said. "How would I know?"

"Yeah," Angelica said, shifting her eyes, "how would we know?"

"I figured one of you knew," I said, "and now I think I know which one."

"What are you talkin' about?" Melissa demanded.

"Before I let you go, Melissa, have you had any dealings with parents?"

"No," Melissa said, "I only interact with teachers, and students."

"Okay, then," I said. "You can go."

Now she looked amused.

"And leave the two of you unchaperoned?" she asked.

"Leave the door open," I suggested. "I think it'll be all right."

Melissa smiled at Angelica and said, "Good luck."

As she went out the door Angelica breathed, "Bitch."

"Angelica," I said, "tell me about Tommy Oronotti."

"I don't know anything about Tommy O," she said.

"You know enough to call him Tommy O," I said.

She hesitated, then said, "You called him that."

"No, I didn't," I said. "Neither time we've spoken."

"Then..." She groped.

"Then maybe Lacy mentioned him?"

"Maybe."

"Good," I said. "That's what I want to know."

"What, exactly?"

"What Lacy said about Tommy O?"

Angelica bit her lip.

"Come on, Angelica," I said. "Can I call you Angie?"

Her eyes flared. "No! Nobody calls me that."

"Okay." I held my hands up in surrender on that point. "Just tell me what you know. Lacy must've talked to you as a friend, or maybe just as a roommate."

"We weren't friends."

I waited a few beats, and then said, "But?"

"She did mention a...Tommy O."

"But she didn't mention his last name?"

"No."

"Okay," I said, "but you knew there was a Tommy O."

"Yes."

"But you never saw him."

"No."

"So when she sneaked him into your room..."

"...I'd go sleep in another room."

"But the night she disappeared, you slept in your own room."

"Yes."

"And did Lacy sleep there?"

"I thought so," she said. "I mean, we both got into our beds, and then...that's all I remember until morning."

"Angelica," I said, "I need you to tell me everything Lacy ever said to you about Tommy O, and then I'll let you go."

She gave it a few moments, scrunching up her pretty face in thought.

"She said he was gonna take her away," she said, finally.

"To where?"

"I don't know," she replied. "She just said he had a place."

"And she didn't say where?"

"No."

"And she said she was going with him?"

She hesitated, then said, "Not in those words."

"What did she say, exactly?"

"She said," Angelica answered, "that he was going to take her away."

"And did she say she wanted to go?"

"She said," Angelica responded slowly, "that she wanted to get away, but she didn't really say with him."

I realized I still had to find out where Tommy lived, go and see his family. The murder of Constance Pennyworth had distracted me from it.

"Before we finish, Angelica," I said, "what did Lacy ever tell you about her parents?"

"She didn't talk about them."

"Never?"

"Never."

"Not her mother, or her father?" I asked. "During parent/ teacher conference week or something?"

"No," she said, shaking her head, "never."

"All right, Angelica," I said. "You can go. Thank you."

She stood and hurried out without looking at me.

I got out my cell and punched in a number. She didn't answer, so I left a message.

"Ally, I assume you're still at the Four Seasons," I said. "When you get back to the office, please find me a home address for any family by the name Oronotti."

FORTY-ONE

When Mrs. Fenster returned I asked to see Lacy's room.

"I can have Melissa take you there," she offered.

"Could someone else do it?"

"Like who, Mr. Headston?"

"Like you, Mrs. Fenster."

Classes were in progress, so the dorm was empty when Mrs. Fenster walked me over.

"This is it," she said, stopping in front of a door.

"Do you want to come in with me?" I asked. "To make sure I don't...take anything?"

"That won't be necessary," she said. "All of Lacy's belongings, and bed, are on the right side. I'll just wait here." She leaned against the wall next to the door and folded her arms. I went inside.

The right side—Lacy's side—was neat as a pin. Meanwhile, the left side looked as if a hurricane had come through the room. There were frilly underthings on the bed and the floor, T-shirts strewn about. I ignored Angelica's side and turned to Lacy's.

I didn't really expect to find anything, but there might have been a note or something helpful there, anything to indicate where she'd gone, and if, indeed, she'd gone on her own.

There was a desk with a laptop on it. I went through the drawers, found nothing, turned on the laptop but didn't know the password to get into it. I went to the door and opened it.

"Helen, do you know the password for her computer?" I asked.

"No, I don't."

"Well," I said, "I haven't found anything, but I'd like to get into her laptop. I have somebody in my office who should be able to do that, so I'd like to take it with me."

"It's private," she said.

"We still don't know if this girl went off of her own volition, or if she was taken. There might be something in her emails to indicate that."

"Very well," she said, "take it."

I went back into the room, came out with the thin laptop under my arm.

"It's an HP," I said. "Do all the girls have these? Are they given to them?"

"No," she said, "it's just like the books, the student has to buy their own."

"Got it."

We left the dorm and stopped just outside.

"Will you need to come back to my office for any reason?" she asked.

"No," I said. "We can go our separate ways right here. I'll just head for the subway."

"Do you go everywhere on the subway?" she asked.

"Usually," I said. "Why?"

"I just thought, you bein' a detective and all that you'd, you know."

"Have a car?" I asked. "Like Mannix?"

"Who?"

"Spenser?"

She shook her head and shrugged.

"Never mind," I said. "Thanks for your help, Helen."

She headed for the main building. I watched her walk for a few minutes, curious about whether she'd turn and look back, but she never did. At least, not while I was watching.

I headed for the subway.

When I got back to the office Ally wasn't there. I couldn't imagine she was still at the Four Seasons—unless she had gotten an offer she couldn't refuse.

But apparently that wasn't the case, because she walked in shortly after I did. She was wearing a jacket-and-slacks business suit, which covered all her tats and made her look very businesslike.

"Well, well, look at you," I said. "I'm impressed."

"Thanks."

"Did you get my message?" I asked.

"I did," she said. "I'm just gettin' back, but I used my phone to get what you wanted, and I emailed the list to you."

"Good."

I went into my office, retrieved Lacy's laptop, and carried it out.

"Is this for me?" she asked, taking it. "A new laptop?"

"No," I said, "it's Lacy Jonkowski's. I need you to crack her password and get into it."

"Okay."

"After you tell me what you found out at the Four Seasons."

"Neither the bartender or the waitress ever saw her in there with a man other than her husband or the lawyer. If she was messin' around, she wasn't doin' it in that hotel."

"She always was careful," I observed.

"You should know," she said, then quickly added, "I'm not judgin', I'm just sayin'."

"Get to work on that laptop," I said.

"What am I lookin' for?"

"Anything that tells us where she went," I said, "and whether or not she went on her own."

"Right. And where are you gonna be?"

"I'll be trying to find out which of these Oronottis you gave me is Tommy O's family."

"And what about the murder case?"

"I'm not investigating a murder case, remember?" I said.

"Then what else will we be doin' to check on Mrs. Pennyworth's, um, extracurricular activities?"

"I'm working on it," I said. "Let me know when you get into that laptop."

"You got it."

I turned and went into my office.

FORTY-TWO

Ally had gotten me five addresses and phone numbers for families named Oronotti. The fourth one I called said yes, they had a Tommy Oronotti in their family. He was sixty-four years old.

On the fifth call a woman said to me, "Oh, you mean Tommy O."

"Yes," I said, "that's right. Is he a young man?"

"He's twenty-two," the woman said.

"Is he around?"

"Around here? Hell, no. We kicked his ass out months ago."

"Oh, I'm sorry," I said. "Are you his mother?"

"No, I'm his grandmother."

"And can I ask, why was he kicked out of the house?"

"Because he thinks he's some kind of Mafia thug," she said. "We don't approve of that, here."

"Then do you know where I can find him?"

"There are still some Italian clubs in Little Italy," she said. "Try there."

"Thank you, Mrs.—" I said, but she hung up.

I checked the address for Tommy O's family, and saw that they lived in Staten Island. The Gambino, Bonanno and Lucchese Families still maintained a presence in Staten Island. I doubted very much that Tommy O had ties to any of them. If he did, Sugar Garbanzo would probably know. At the moment Sugar's own ties—no matter how "legitimate" he claimed to be—were with the Lucchese Family. If he knew that Tommy O had a family connection, he would have taken care of it through channels, and not hired me.

I still wasn't really sure why he had hired me, but there were some pieces of this puzzle that were rattling around in my head, and I thought I knew just the person who could fit them together for me.

I took a business card from my wallet and dialed the number on my cell. When it was answered I made an appointment for later that day—in only an hour.

"I'll be back," I said, on my way past Ally's desk.

When I got to the office of Chase, Meyer and Walcott I found my way to Winston Chase's office and presented myself to his well-turned-out blond secretary.

"Oh yes, Mr....Headstone?"

"Headston."

"That's right, Headston," she said. She hit a switch and said, "Mr. Headston is here."

"Send him in."

She smiled at me. "You can go in."

"Thank you."

I entered Chase's office as he stood up from his desk. Through the window behind him I could see several high rises.

"Mr. Headston," he said. He remained behind the desk, so I had to reach across to shake his hand. "Have a seat, please. Tell me what I can do for you."

"You can tell me what your connection is to Sugar Garbanzo."

His face went stiff.

"Excuse me?"

"Dominick 'Sugar' Garbanzo," I said, slowly.

"How did you come across that name?" he asked.

"Sugar and me, we went to high school together," I said.

"His daughter's missing from her school and he asked me to look into it. Guess what I found out? You're her ersatz daddy."

"Her...ersatz..."

"You registered her," I said. "Why?"

He squared his shoulders and said, "Mr. Garbanzo is a client. He tasked me with registering the girl in St. Mary's."

"Without letting them know who her father was, right?"

"Correct," Chase said. "It wasn't so much that he didn't want the school to know who he was, he doesn't want the girl to know he's her father."

"Why'd you register her as Jonkowski?"

"Because he told me that was her last name."

"And told me her mother was Mary-Ann Jonkowski. But we both went to school with her, and when I asked she denied it."

"Why would you be working on this instead of Constance Pennyworth's murder?" he asked.

I held up my forefinger. "I'm not working the murder, remember?"

"Be that as it may, tracking her movements still takes precedence over a missing girl who, frankly, may not really be missing."

"So you've talked with Sugar about this?"

"No, uh, well..."

"Mr. Chase," I said, "I can't help thinking that your connection to Sugar also suggests a connection between Sugar and Alan Pennyworth."

"Well...they're both clients of my firm, but—"

"Do they know each other?"

Chase hesitated, then said, "I don't believe so."

"You don't believe so?" I asked. "You're very good at this, aren't you, Mr. Chase?"

"At what?"

"At being a mob lawyer."

"I'm not..." He stopped, firmed his jaw.

"Why do I get the feeling I'm being played?" I asked. "Sugar comes out of nowhere and hires me to find his daughter just when Constance Pennyworth is killed. Was he trying to keep me off the Pennyworth case?"

"Headston—"

"And if so, why? Who's he trying to protect? Your client, Alan?"

"I don't know what you're—"

I stood up.

"I think I have enough on both cases," I said. "Thanks very much."

"Headston!" He jumped up from his desk and followed me out of his office. "Headston, wait. You don't understand."

"Sure I do," I said. "I'm being played on both ends. And you're the connection. Thank you."

I stormed out.

FORTY-THREE

Chase was probably going to call both his clients, so I hotfooted it over to the Four Seasons to try to catch Alan Pennyworth in his suite. When I banged on the door to his room, he opened it immediately.

"I've been expecting you," he said, allowing me to enter. "Drink?"

"I don't need a drink," I said, following him into the room. "I need some answers."

"To what questions?" he asked.

"Did you kill your wife?"

Pennyworth was in the act of sitting on the sofa, and stopped, staring at me.

"That's quite a question," he said, then sat. "What makes you ask it?"

"Steps have apparently been taken to distract me from this case," I said.

"By whom?"

"By a friend of yours."

"What friend of mine would go to such lengths—"

"Sugar Garbanzo."

"Suga—oh, you mean Dominick Garbanzo?"

"Yes."

"Isn't he a gangster?" he asked, after a pregnant pause. "Why would I be friends with a gangster?"

"He has some legitimate business interests, as well," I explained.

"Not with me, he doesn't," he responded, firmly. "And why would you think this means I killed Constance?"

"Why else have me distracted from my investigation?"

"That makes no sense. If I killed her," he said, "why would I hire you?"

"To make it look like you didn't," I said. "You would especially want your family, your daughters, to be convinced that you didn't do it."

"This all sounds excruciatingly convoluted," he said. "If I killed Constance, I would simply sit back and let the police investigate. I would not hire an old boyfriend to look into the matter."

That caused me to pause.

"Boyfriend?" I asked.

"Certainly," he said. "You don't think for a moment I didn't know about you and Constance—that is, Carla, as she was called back then."

"You knew about that?"

"Before I married Constance I had her thoroughly investigated...by a good private investigator, by the way."

Ouch.

"Thoroughly?"

"Oh yes," he said, "I knew about her dubious background as a con woman and adulteress."

"And you married her, anyway?"

"I was in love with her," he said, "and as long as I knew everything, there was no harm."

He ran his fingers along the crease of his right pant leg, then crossed it over his left and sipped from his drink. He was so nonchalant I thought he might fall asleep.

I felt sure, at that point, he had killed Constance.

But why would he think that sending me after a missing girl

would be enough to distract me from a murder (which I, techni-cally, wasn't investigating)? Was it because it was Sugar Garbanzo hiring me? Did they think I'd be that afraid of Sugar?

"You did it, didn't you?" I asked.

"You'll have to prove that," he said, without bothering to deny it. "Oh wait, you're not permitted to work on an open homicide case, are you?"

"I'll talk to the cops, anyway."

"And risk losing your license again?" he asked, shaking his head. "Oh yes, when investigating Constance, I found out how she destroyed your life."

"You're depending on me not wanting to destroy my life again, to allow you to get away with murder?"

"Again," he said, "prove it."

"How about Sugar?" I asked. "Does he know you're using him to try to cover up a murder?"

"Mr. Garbanzo and I have done some business," he said. "That's all."

"And your daughters?" I asked. "Do they know about this business? Oh wait, they didn't like Constance. They're probably glad she's—well, gone." Suddenly, something very Agatha Christie occurred to me. "Was this a family thing?" I asked. "Like *Murder on the Orient Express*? Did you all do it?"

"Mr. Headston," Pennyworth said, uncrossing his legs, "I think we're done. You can consider yourself discharged, no longer in my employ or that of Winston Chase."

"You haven't seen the last of me," I said.

"Idle threats do not impress me, sir." He waved, looking away from me, his gaze drifting out the window. "Feel free to see yourself out."

I left the suite in a foul mood. Was I prepared to toss another bomb into the center of my life? To get the man who killed the woman who tossed the first bomb?

The people in the lobby seemed to sense my mood. Either that, or my stride and the look on my face was plainly projecting it.

They parted like the Red Sea and I went out the door and headed for the subway. My intention was to get back to my office and do some heavy thinking.

I had almost made it to the subway entrance when a black van pulled up to the curb. Three men wearing ski masks jumped out, and before I knew what they doing, had tossed me into the back of the van. Once there, somebody hit me on the head, and I was out.

FORTY-FOUR

I woke up in a dark room, tied to a chair. I know this happens to TV detectives a lot, but this was my first experience. It was complete with the concrete floor, the single bare bulb above my head and the sound of water dripping somewhere, almost as if it had been set up.

Also on TV the private eye would start yelling, "Hello! Hello! Is anybody there?" I didn't. I assumed whoever took me would come in and talk to me eventually, otherwise why tie me up? They could've just killed me if they wanted me out of the way.

I didn't know how long I had been there, and I think I passed out a time or two (I won't say I fell asleep, because that would make me sound much too cool about the situation). But a door finally opened and the first thing I saw was a glimpse of crimson, then Sugar appeared, carrying a bottle of water. Behind him came two other hulks, dressed in jeans and T-shirts.

"Untie his hands," Sugar ordered.

One of the hulks came over and did so, and then Sugar handed the other one the bottle of water and told him to give it to me. I accepted it and drank down half, I was so thirsty. If I was drugged, so be it.

One of the hulks brought another chair over and set it about ten feet in front of me. Sugar sat and stared at me.

"Johnny," he said, "we're friends."

"Are we?" I asked, after clearing my throat. "Were we ever friends, Dom?"

"There you go," he said. "Nobody but an old friend would call me 'Dom.'"

"Fine," I relented, "let's say we've both agreed that we're friends. Now what?"

"Well," he said, "you messed up."

"You lied to me, Dom," I said. "Friends don't do that. In fact, friends don't throw their friends into a damp basement. This is all very dramatic."

"Johnny," Sugar said, "I'm just tryin' to make a point."

"Well, make it," I said. "I'm hungry and I need a shower."

"Damn it, Johnny," Sugar said, "you're gonna make this hard." He nodded, and before I could speak one of the hulks stepped in and hit me in the face with a first like a ham. It knocked me off the chair and before I could get comfortable on the floor, the other hulk picked me up and put me back in the chair.

"How's that for drama?" Sugar asked.

I used my tongue to check if I had all my teeth, spit blood onto the floor and said, "Get to the point, Dom. Do you even have a daughter?"

"Of course I do," he said. "Do you think I got that school to go along with a lie? Lacy really is there as a student, and she did take off with Tommy O, but I'm gonna take care of that."

"And Mary-Ann?"

"I just needed a last name for Lacy when I registered her in the school," he said. "And I figured I could convince you that Mary-Ann was the liar."

"And this was all supposed to distract me from the murder of Constance Pennyworth."

"My lawyer, Winston Chase, asked me for a favor, and since he helped me when I wanted to put Lacy in that school, I said okay. And I was sure I could handle you, because—well, let's face it, I did in high school. And people don't really change much."

"That's where you went wrong," I said.

"I guess. So now we're here."

"Sugar," I said, "you're helping Pennyworth cover up a murder."

"Big shocker," Sugar said. "A rich man kills his wife. Get over it, John."

"Okay, so your little Lacy problem didn't get the job done," I said. "Now what? Did Pennyworth order you to kill me?"

"Well...yeah," Sugar said. "I mean, no, he didn't order me to kill you, but he asked me to "

"Sugar, Sugar," I said, shaking my head, "friends don't kill friends, man."

Don't get the wrong idea. I was scared. I didn't know if Sugar would kill me himself, or have his hulks do it, but I felt like my window for talking him out of it was closing.

"Okay," he said, jumping to his feet.

"Okay, what?" I asked, as they retied my hands.

"I'm gonna let you think things over for a while," Sugar said, "and then I'm gonna come back and ask you a question. Dependin' on the answer, you'll either walk out of here or..."

"Or what?"

"...or you won't."

FORTY-FIVE

Okay, this time I did fall asleep. But I was still scared. I kept wondering when Sugar was going to come in and ask his question, and whether or not he'd have his two hulks with him.

I lost track of how long I was there. Would Ally have gotten worried by now? Would she call the police? And what good would that do? There was no way they'd figure out where I was.

Unless we were followed, and what were the chances of that?

When the door opened again Sugar came in clad in a blue running suit. But there was no one with him this time. I didn't know if that was good or bad.

"Where are your buddies?" I asked.

He came around behind me, untied my hands and handed me another bottle of water.

"I don't need them for this," he said, coming around in front of me.

"For what?" I asked, after drinking half the bottle.

"I've got a question to ask you," he said.

"Then ask," I said, "Let's get this over with. I've got work to do, and my secretary is probably worried about me."

"Johnny," he said. "what do you intend to do about the dead woman, Constance Pennyworth?"

"It's a police matter, Dom," I said. "All I can do is tell them what I know, and what I suspect."

"And what's that?"

"You know what it is," I said. "Pennyworth killed his wife. That's why he's had you grab me off the street."

"What?" Sugar asked. "Pennyworth didn't tell me any such thing."

"Then why am I here?" I demanded.

"I don't take orders from Alan Pennyworth," Sugar went on. "We're on the same board of some business, is all."

"Then who told you to snatch me off the street?"

"That's not important," Sugar said. "What I have to figure out is what to do with you."

"I thought the plan was to kill me."

"Yeah, it was," Sugar said, "but that was for the benefit of those other two mugs."

"Aren't they your men?" I asked.

"They're Lucchese men."

"Aren't you a Lucchese man, Sugar?"

"When it suits me," Sugar said, "and right now it doesn't."

"Why not?"

"Because they want you dead," he said. "I told you, we're friends, Johnny. I don't kill my friends."

"So where does that leave us, Dom?"

"Right now," he answered in a whisper, "that leaves you escaping..."

Sugar showed me the way out, but he wouldn't give me a gun.

"I've gotta have—whatta the spies call it?—deniability. If you get away, fine, but if you kill somebody, there's gonna be a stink about where you got a gun."

"Well," I said, "thanks for letting me go."

"I didn't let you go," he said. "You escaped."

"Right. Will you be in trouble when I go to the cops?" I asked.

"Naw, don't worry about me," he said. "I'll be fine."

"And your daughter?"

"I know where she is, Johnny," he said, looking sheepish. "I'll handle it. Now go. And watch your ass around that lawyer, Chase."

"Why?"

"Because he's more than just a lawyer."

He showed me to a long, dark hallway, and slammed the metal door shut behind me. I was in the dark, figuratively and literally. Was he sending me down this hall to get killed? Or was he really helping me get away because we were "friends?"

Only one way to find out.

I allowed my eyes to adjust and when I was able to make out the walls and the floor—there wasn't much else—I headed down the hall. It was damp, and there were no doors along the way. But when I came around a bend I saw an outline of light that I assumed would be a doorway. I increased my pace, even though I heard no one behind me.

When I reached the light I'd seen it was, indeed, a door. As I felt around for a handle or a knob I could feel that it was metal. What the hell kind of bunker had Sugar and his goons taken me to?

I finally encountered a handle and pulled it. The door was unlocked, and opened. The light seared my eyes and I backed up for a minute, letting the door close again. I waited a moment, listening for anyone coming down the hall behind me. Hearing no one, I opened the door again, this time slowly. The sun was quite bright, indicating it was probably the middle of the day.

Finally, I stepped outside, because I couldn't afford to wait much longer. Sugar's goons would realize I was gone eventually, and start looking.

Squinting against the sun I walked away from the door, then turned to look at it. It looked as if it was set into the side of a hill. I actually had been inside some kind of a bunker.

I looked around, saw a lot of land and trees, and not much

else. I didn't know where the hell I was, but I had to put some distance between myself and that bunker, so I started walking.

Eventually I spotted something I knew. I walked towards it, and found myself standing at the water's edge, staring across at the skyline of Manhattan, and to the left at the George Washington Bridge. I was where I very rarely have reason or desire to go.

New Jersey.

I was in a field in northern New Jersey, and to my north would be the city of Fort Lee. I needed to find my way to a highway, where I could hitch a ride. But I wasn't that familiar with New Jersey because, as I said, I rarely went there. With the Hudson River in front of me, I had to turn and start walking the opposite way.

FORTY-SIX

It was almost midnight when I walked into my apartment. It took me that long to find a road, catch a ride, get to Fort Lee, and then get a ride to Manhattan. I couldn't take a cab because I didn't have my wallet or any cash on me. I flagged a couple, but they didn't buy that I'd pay them when we reached our destination. I finally flagged a ride across the GW with a trucker. He let me off where I was able to get to the subway and take the train home.

I poured myself a stiff shot of whiskey, with the intention of taking a shower right after. However, before I could finish the drink my doorbell sounded. I didn't live in a building with a doorman, or with an electronic front door, so it could've been anybody. When I looked through the peephole I saw Ally standing there.

In talking to the truck driver I realized I had been gone two days. Ally was probably worried, and decided to check and see if I was home.

I opened the door and she looked at me, startled, and said, "I'm sorry, Johnny."

"For what?"

She looked ashamed when the two goons stepped into view, both holding guns.

"We been waitin' for you," one of them said.

It was the same two guys who had held me in the bunker with Sugar.

"They were waiting downstairs," she said.

"For you," the spokesman said. "But this pretty little thing came along, so we grabbed her, too." He prodded her. "Inside."

"You think I'm pretty?" she asked him.

The other man pushed her and said, "Inside."

I stepped back so Ally could enter, followed by the two gunmen.

"We don't know how you got out," the first gunman said, "but we figured you'd come home."

"So you're going to kill me in my own home?"

"I guess so," he said. "You should've stayed with us in Jersey. It would've been cleaner, and easier."

"What are your names?" I asked.

"I'm Clark," the first man said, "and that's Henry."

Not exactly the name you'd expect from a couple of knuckle draggers.

"Does Sugar know you're here?" I asked.

"He knows," Clark said. "Henry, look around. Make sure nobody else is here before we do this."

"Okay."

"You two sit down," Clark said to Ally and me.

We sat together on the sofa.

"So that's where you've been for two days?" she asked me. "In New Jersey?"

"In some kind of a bunker," I said. "These guys work for Sugar."

"Why'd they grab you?"

"I figured out that Alan Pennyworth actually killed his wife," I said.

"What about Sugar's daughter?"

"That was just something to distract me from the murder."

"Shut up, both of you," Clark said. "Henry!"

Henry came running back in.

"Nobody else here," he said.

"Did you find a gun?"

Henry looked confused.

"You didn't say anythin' about lookin' for no gun."

Clark rolled his eyes.

"I'll go look now," Henry offered.

"Never mind!" Clark said. "We'll just shoot 'em and get it over with."

"Right."

We all looked at Henry, whose hand was empty.

"Where's your gun?" Clark asked.

"I, uh, put it down when I was in the kitchen."

"Why?"

"Um, I looked in the refrigerator." Henry looked abashed. "I'm hungry."

Clark looked at me, as if for support.

"Sorry," I said, "I don't keep much in there."

"I know!" Henry said, disapprovingly. "A jar of pickles, a box of baking soda, and a container of milk—expired!"

"The baking soda keeps the expired milk from smelling up the fridge," I explained.

"Does that really work?" Ally asked.

"No," I said.

She took my hands, and I could feel her clammy palm. She was scared. That made two of us.

"Go and get your gun, Henry," Clark said. "I ain't doin' this myself."

"Yeah, right."

Henry rushed back to the kitchen.

"I can't find it!" he shouted, moments later.

Clark looked at me again, helplessly.

"Tell him to look in the refrigerator," Ally suggested.

"That's helpful," I said.

"Sorry," she said. "I'm scared."

"So am I."

She looked at the front door. I'd noticed she kept looking over at it.

"Don't," I said. "If you run they'll shoot."

"If we sit here they'll shoot," she reasoned.

"Here it is!" Henry came into the room, carrying his gun. "It was in the refrigerator."

"Well, it better work," Clark said.

Henry came over and stood next to his partner. They looked like matching hulks. I hated that they might be the last thing I saw.

"Let the girl go, guys," I said. "She's not part of this."

"She is now."

They straightened their arms, pointing their guns at us. I prepared myself to jump up off the couch. Maybe I could do something to help Ally get away. Before I could move she jumped to her feet, waved her arms and started yelling. Both men stared at her like she'd gone crazy.

That was when something slammed into the door, and it burst open.

FORTY-SEVEN

Two uniformed police officers stumbled in, preceded by a port-
able battering ram. Behind them came Detectives Leon and
Stokes, guns in hand.

"Hold it there!" Leon shouted at the two goons.

Clark and Henry couldn't decide whether to keep their guns
pointed at me, or whirl around and point them at the police.
When the two uniforms regained their balance and took out
their Glocks, the two hulks realized they were outgunned.

"Drop 'em!" Leon shouted.

They could've just shot me, but that would've been commit-
ting murder right in front of the police, so they released their
guns and let them hit the floor. Moments later they were being
led to the door in cuffs.

"Hold on," Ally said.

The cops stopped, and the two cuffed men turned. Ally stepped
in and punched Clark right in the face then turned and said to
me, "He pinched my butt."

Stokes and Leon both shrugged and looked at me.

"Thank you, Detectives," I said. "I don't know how you
knew—"

"Thank your girl, here," Stokes said. "She came here to see if
you were home, and saw these two out front. Then she was
smart enough to call us."

"She called us when you went missing," Leon added, "so we figured we'd better get over here."

"Well," I said, "then I appreciate all three of you."

"Maybe of the three of us," Ally said, "I can get a raise?"

I looked at her and said, "Maybe."

"Let's go," Leon said to me. "We're gonna need a statement about where you've been and what this was about."

"He's a mess, Detective," Ally said. "Can he change first?"

"Sure," Leon said. "I'll leave a car downstairs to drive you over when you're ready."

"Thanks."

They left the apartment, which now had a broken front door.

"Ally, can you call someone to fix that door while I go and get changed?"

"Sure," she said, "but you better take a quick shower, too. You stink."

"There's a police car waiting downstairs for me," I said.

"Let 'em wait."

I walked into One Police Plaza an hour later, and they put me right in an interrogation room. Leon and Stokes sat with me while I explained both cases, Pennyworth and Sugar Garbanzo's, and how they were related.

When I was done the two detectives exchanged a glance.

"What's wrong?" I asked. "What is it?"

"We've had two bodies in the last two days, and we thought they were both mob hits," Stokes said.

"Who's dead?" I asked.

"First," Leon said, "A kid named Tommy Oronotti, also known as Tommy O."

"The boy Lacy ran away with. How was he killed?"

"Shot."

"Did you find Lacy?"

"She's back at the school," Stokes said.

"And the second body?"

They both hesitated, then Stokes said, "Sugar Garbanzo. Also shot."

"He was a friend of yours," Leon said. "Sorry."

"He must've been killed earlier today," I said, "after he let me escape. They must've figured it out."

"Who they?" Stokes asked. "Clark and Henry?"

"I'm sure they did it, before they came to get me," I said. "But they had orders."

"From who?" Leon asked. "Somebody in the Lucchese Family?"

"This wasn't mob business," I said. "The only connections to the Lucchese Family is the lawyer, Chase, but he's also Alan Pennyworth's lawyer."

"So you think Pennyworth killed his wife, and hired you to give himself some kind of an alibi," Leon said.

"Yeah, along with the phony attempts on him three months ago. Only he didn't hire me then, Constance did. She brought me into the whole thing."

"But he was already plannin' on killin' her," Leon said.

"Yeah," I said. "He probably put it off, wanting to get a little distance from my involvement."

"And then he dragged you right back in," Stokes said.

"Only because I showed up," I said. "He made a snap decision, one he probably regretted. So he contacted Sugar to do something to distract me."

"Not realizing that you and Garbanzo knew each other," Leon said.

"I guess not. But once I found the link between Pennyworth and Sugar, which was Chase, I went right to Pennyworth, and he must've put the word out on me as soon as I left his suite, because they got me before I reached the subway."

"Headston," Stokes said, "you got any proof that Pennyworth killed his wife?"

"No," I said, "but you've got Clark and Henry, who must've

killed Sugar on Chase's word."

"What makes you say that?"

"When Sugar let me go he told me to watch out for Chase, that he was more than just a lawyer."

"We've suspected that about Chase for a while," Stokes said.

"But I don't know if these two goons are gonna give us Chase."

"There may be another way to go," I suggested.

"Howzat?" Leon asked.

"I don't think any of this has anything to do with the Lucchese Family," I said. "And I don't think they're going to like having their names connected to two murders."

"So we just need to hold that over their heads," Leon said.

"That's what I'm saying."

"I guess we'll try that," Stokes said, "but Headston, we're not thrilled with the fact that you were working the Pennyworth murder, even if your information does lead us to Pennyworth as the culprit."

"I was working on her last hours—" I started, but they cut me off.

"Forget that," Leon said. "We're not going to come down on you for this, not if it leads to Pennyworth. And whoever killed Sugar."

"Then can I go?" I asked. "I'm sort of wiped out."

"What about the missing girl?" Stokes asked.

"Sugar told me she's back," I said. "I think you're going to find she's back because he had Tommy O whacked."

"And are we sure this girl actually was Sugar's daughter?"

"Supposedly his and a girl named Mary-Ann Jonkowski's, but so much of that was lies I'm not even sure."

"Well," Leon said, "if she's back, she's back. We're more concerned with these homicides."

"I'm looking at Clark and Henry," I said. "I figure Sugar had them kill Tommy O, and then Chase had them kill Sugar."

"And the only way we're gonna prove any of this is to have them flip on Chase."

"And have Chase flip on Pennyworth," I said.

Leon shook his head and said, "Convoluted. I like when husbands and wives kill each other for obvious reasons and we solve the case in two days."

"Yeah, well," I said, "I like to stay out of murders, myself."

"Good," Stokes said. "Just keep thinkin' that way."

"Go home, Headston," Leon said. "I know it's no use tellin' you this, but stay outta trouble."

I found Ally waiting for me down in the lobby.

"Why didn't you go home?" I asked.

"I figured if I let you get on the subway alone you'd fall asleep until the last stop."

I yawned and said, "You might be right. although I did manage to catch a few winks in that bunker."

"What kinda bunker was it?"

"I have no idea. It was south of Fort Lee, might've been built by somebody in the sixties, when they had kids ducking under their desks in school to avoid the atom bomb, or something. All I care about is I got out, thanks to Sugar."

"And now he's dead?"

"Yeah," I said, "and pretty much because he considered us friends."

"And you didn't?"

"I don't stay in touch with people I went to school with," I said. "And I can count my real friends on the fingers of one hand. Sugar was...well, Sugar. To my way of thinking, just somebody I knew once."

"And Carla?" she asked.

"Carla...well, Carla was just a mistake," I said. "A big mistake." I took her arm. "Let's go."

We went out the front door and headed for the subway.

FORTY-EIGHT

It hadn't escaped my attention that Ally had saved my life. She was a smart girl, and I decided to reward her, not so much with a raise, but with more work outside the office.

That's why when I looked up from my desk and saw Angela Wayne standing there, I was surprised. Ally was out, and hadn't been able to announce her arrival.

"Mrs. Wayne," I said.

"Mr. Headston," she said. "There are so many desks out here for a one-man operation."

"It wasn't always like that," I said. "What can I do for you?"

She entered the office and I noticed that her hair and clothes were different—more expensive, and younger. A skirt that stopped several inches above the knee showed off some fine legs.

"May I sit?" she asked.

"Please."

She settled into the visitor's chair in front of my desk and crossed those excellent gams.

"I suppose you've heard the police arrested my father for killing Constance."

I had read that in the paper, and saw it on television, last week. It had now been two weeks since I'd escaped from that New Jersey bunker.

"I heard."

"And the word I got is that you had something to do with it."

I studied her for a moment. If that was the word she got, she didn't seem upset about it.

"Angela—"

"Don't get me wrong," she said. "If he killed her, he should go to jail."

"If?"

"Well, there's going to be a trial," she said, "but Winston Chase won't be able to defend him, because he got arrested, too, as a mob lawyer."

"I also heard that."

"And I also heard you had something to do with it."

"Since your father killed Constance—allegedly, of course—I simply gave all my findings to the police. If they acted on them, then I guess it's true, I had something to do with each arrest."

"Well, you did me and my sister Sarah a big favor."

"Did I?"

"Yes," she said, "we wanted Constance out of the way—out of the will, if you will." She smiled at her little joke.

This was a different Angela than I had seen before.

"Angela," I said, "what actually brings you here?"

She stood up and walked to my window, which looked down onto Fifth Avenue, then turned and looked at me.

"He didn't do it."

"What?"

"My father didn't kill Constance."

"How do you know that?"

"I can't tell you how I know," she said, "I can only tell you he didn't. And yet...I think he'll be convicted, don't you?"

"I do," I said. "I think even if a jury doesn't believe he did it himself, they'll think he had it done, along with his mob lawyer, Winston Chase."

"And so I thank you," she said. "Constance is gone, my father will be gone, Winston Chase will be gone, and Sarah and I will inherit. All's well that ends well."

"But is it?" I asked.

She stared at me. If she was serious about knowing her father was innocent, did that mean she knew who did it? Or she did it, herself?

"Angela—"

She put her finger to her lips, then walked to my office door and looked out. Satisfied we were alone, she turned back.

"Mr. Headston...can I call you Johnny?"

"Sure, why not?" I asked.

She came back to the chair, crossed her legs again and seemed pleased with herself.

"I did it."

"What?"

"I killed Constance—or the woman you knew as Carla."

"You knew about that?"

She nodded.

"My father had her investigated before he married her. I found the report in his briefcase, one day." She giggled. "I'm a snoop, you see."

I didn't like the giggle. It hinted at something going on beneath the surface, that might be ready to come bubbling—or bursting—out.

"So you knew she had a past as a con woman."

"And I knew what she did to you," she said. "You poor man. You can't be sorry she's dead."

"I don't wish anybody dead, Angela."

"So when you handed the police my father on a silver platter, they never suspected you?"

"No."

"Do they know about her past?"

"They will, before the case is closed," I said.

"Ooh, they might be pissed at you for not coming clean about your history with her."

"They might," I said. "That will remain to be seen. Meanwhile, are you sure you want to confess to me?"

"Why not?" she asked, standing up again. "We're here alone, it'd be your word against mine." She shrugged. "If you even believe me."

"There is that," I said. "After all, why confess?"

"Simple," she said. "I want the credit. I just had to tell somebody."

"So why me?"

"Honestly? As far as I'm concerned, you're a nobody. And given your past with Constance—Carla—I don't think you'd want the case to be wide open, again."

"So you think in light of your confession that I'd just let an innocent man pay for a crime he didn't commit."

"Like I said," she replied, with a shrug, "even if you believe me."

"What about the other attempts on your father?" I asked. "Was that you?"

"That was my dad," she said. "You see, I think he was planning to kill her. I just got there first."

"And what about the attempts on Sarah?"

"That was nonsense!" she spit. "Sarah overreacts."

"She seemed to think her husband wanted her dead."

"It doesn't matter now," she said. "They're separated, headed for divorce."

"Where is she?"

"Staying with me and Harrison."

"You're still with your husband?"

"Oh, yes," she said. "He gives me what I want when I want it, if you know what I mean?"

"You look like money all of a sudden, Angela," I said. "If you think you're going to inherit, it'll still be a while, won't it?"

"Maybe, maybe not," she said. "My dad's almost eighty. If they don't execute him, he'll probably die in jail. And besides, with him locked away somebody has to be in charge of the business."

"You?"

She grinned.

"Me," she said, happily. "Which means I have access to all the accounts."

"So it worked out just the way you wanted it to."

"Pretty much," she said. "I would have preferred that he killed her, but I went up there to see him, and she just pissed me off with her attitude."

"So you strangled her."

"She turned her back, and I snapped. But like I said, all's well that ends well."

"I could still go to the police," I said.

"Go ahead. Like I said, it'd be your word against mine. And you're the one who gave them my dad." She walked to the door, then stopped and turned back. "I don't think we ever need to talk again, do you?"

"There is one more thing," I said.

"What's that?"

"Why the hell would your father confess?"

"Because," she said, "the old fool wants to protect me. After all, I am his daughter."

She waved and left before I could respond. I heard the front door open and close, then heard another open and close.

"Who's there?" I called.

Ally appeared in the doorway, and I knew she had come out of the bathroom. She looked at me, smiled and wiggled her eyebrows.

"She's kinda crazy, don't you think?"

"Did you hear all of it?"

"Oh yeah, I came in, heard her talking and ducked into the bathroom before she started her confession. Because she wanted the credit? That's nuts."

"I think you're right."

"About what?"

"Nuts."

"Do you think she was serious?"

"That's not for me to find out," I said, "it's for the police."

"So you're gonna tell 'em what she said?"

"Why not?" I asked. "It's not her word against mine anymore, is it?"

"And what about you and Carla?" she asked. "Will that have to come out?"

"I'm sure it will," I said. If I turned Angela in, she was sure to blab about my past with Carla. "I'll just have to deal with that when the time comes."

ROBERT J. RANDISI is the author of the "Miles Jacoby," "Nick Delvecchio," "Gil & Claire Hunt," "Dennis McQueen," "Joe Keough," and "The Rat Pack," mystery series. He is the editor of over 30 anthologies. All told he is the author of over 600 novels.

Randisi is the founder of the Private Eye Writers of America, the creator of the Shamus Award, the co-founder of Mystery Scene Magazine.

DOWN & OUT BOOKS

On the following pages are a few
more great titles from the
Down & Out Books publishing family.

For a complete list of books and to
sign up for our newsletter,
go to DownAndOutBooks.com.

ALL DUE RESPECT   SHOTGUN HONEY

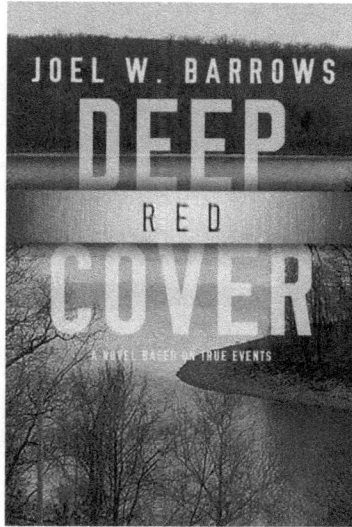

Deep Red Cover
A Cover Thriller
Joel W. Barrows

Down & Out Books
September 2020
978-1-64396-117-0

A body is found on the shores of a Missouri lake, throat slashed. There are few clues, and the trail grows cold for Investigator Morgan Kern.

At the same time, ATF has become increasingly concerned about the growing militia movement. Special Agent David Ward goes undercover to investigate possible illegal weapons trafficking.

Their paths will intersect in a way that neither could have imagined.

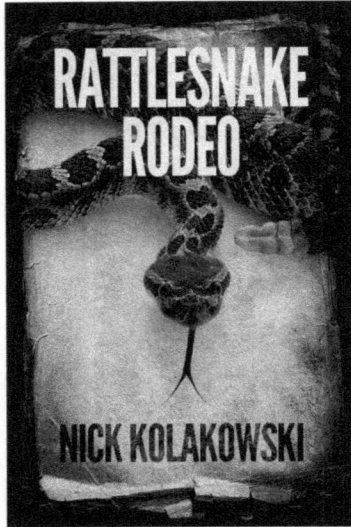

Rattlesnake Rodeo
A Boise Longpig Hunting Club Thriller
Nick Kolakowski

Down & Out Books
October 2020
978-1-64396-128-6

The fiery sequel to *Boise Longpig Hunting Club* is here...

Jake Halligan and his ultra-lethal sister Frankie have survived the Boise Longpig Hunting Club. What comes next, though, might prove far worse.

With the law closing in, they'll have to make the hardest choices if they want to survive.

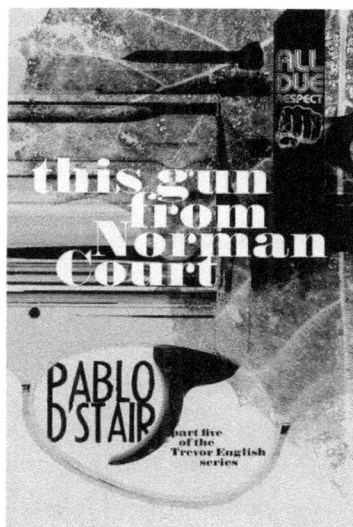

this gun from Norman Court
The Trevor English Series
Pablo D'Stair

All Due Respect, an imprint of
Down & Out Books
October 2020
978-1-64396-119-4

Reduced to life in skid-row shelters, petty thief Trevor English is apprehended by store-detective-cum-freelance-investigator Leonard Bellow. Turning a blind eye to his theft, Bellow offers Trevor a job doing reconnaissance work – an opportunity Trevor jumps at.

But in the world he has cornered himself in nothing is what it seems on the surface … except, he will realize, for Trevor English: deadbeat, easy mark, lamb to the slaughter.

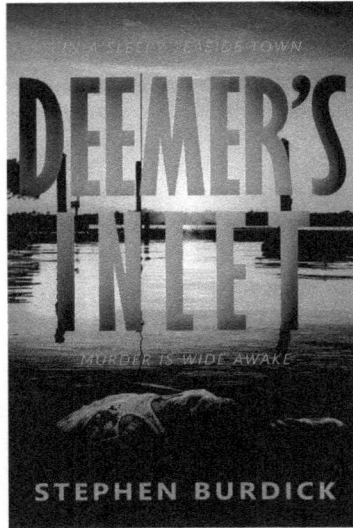

Deemer's Inlet
Stephen Burdick

Shotgun Honey, an imprint of
Down & Out Books
August 2020
978-1-64396-104-0

Far from the tourist meccas of Ft. Lauderdale and Miami Beach, a chief of police position in the quiet, picturesque town of Deemer's Inlet on the Gulf coast of Florida seemed ideal for Eldon Quick—until the first murder.

The crime and a subsequent killing force Quick to call upon his years of experience as a former homicide detective in Miami. Soon after, two more people are murdered and Quick believes a serial killer is on the loose. As Quick works to uncover the identity and motive of the killer, he must contend with an understaffed police force, small town politics, and curious residents.

www.ingramcontent.com/pod-product-compliance
Lightning Source LLC
Chambersburg PA
CBHW020253030426
42336CB00010B/747